HORSE & PONY BOOK

CAROLYN HENDERSON

A DORLING KINDERSLEY BOOK

LONDON, NEW YORK, MUNICH,
PARIS, MELBOURNE, DELHI

Editor Clare Lister
Designer Joanne Little
Jacket Design Neal Cobourne
Design Manager Jane Thomas
Category Publisher Sue Grabham
With thanks to the original team:
Project Editor Claire Bampton
Project Art Editor Lesley Betts
Photography Andy Crawford and John Henderson

This edition Published 2008
by Dorling Kindersley Limited,
80 Strand, London WC2R 0RL
A Penguin company

A CIP catalogue record for this book is available from
the British Library.

ISBN 978-0-7513-4399-1

Colour reproduction by Colourscan, Singapore

Printed and bound in China

See our complete catalogue at www.dk.com

CONTENTS

Improve Your Riding Skills

Horse and Pony Care

Horse and Pony Breeds

Shows and Events

IMPROVE YOUR
RIDING
SKILLS

GETTING STARTED

THE BEST PLACE to learn to ride a pony is at a good riding school. Here there are experienced instructors who have been trained to work with novice riders. They are familiar with the most suitable horses and ponies on which to learn, so your lessons will be safe and enjoyable. Try to have a lesson at least once a week – more often if you have the chance.

Instructor leads pony while you ride.

Ready to ride

Dress safely and comfortably for your lessons. Always wear a hat or helmet that meets the highest safety standards. Many schools will lend you one at first, but eventually you will need to buy your own. Never buy a secondhand hat, since it may have been damaged in a fall. Jodhpurs or comfortable trousers and riding boots or safe shoes are also essential.

Hat must fit properly.

Always fasten the safety harness.

YOUR INSTRUCTOR
During the first few lessons, your instructor will lead your pony using either a lead rein or a long lunge rein. This allows you to concentrate on sitting correctly and getting used to the feel of riding.

Horse should be in good condition – neither too fat nor too thin.

Tack should fit the horse well and be correctly adjusted.

Stirrup irons must be the correct size, so your feet cannot slide through or become trapped.

Long rubber riding boots or short jodhpur boots are suitable for beginners.

Horse should be well shod.

THE RIGHT PONY
Your instructor will choose a horse or pony for your lessons that is the right size for you. It should be quiet, friendly, and reliable and be used to being ridden and handled by beginners.

Choosing a riding school

Friends who are also learning to ride may recommend suitable schools. Local vets, saddlers, and riding club or pony club officials may also have addresses of suitable establishments. Visit a school before arranging any lessons and check that it seems well-run. Horses should be in good condition and the staff friendly and helpful.

THE STABLE YARD

The yard should be tidy, with tools and equipment stored safely. There should be an enclosed riding arena (manege). Some schools may also have indoor arenas.

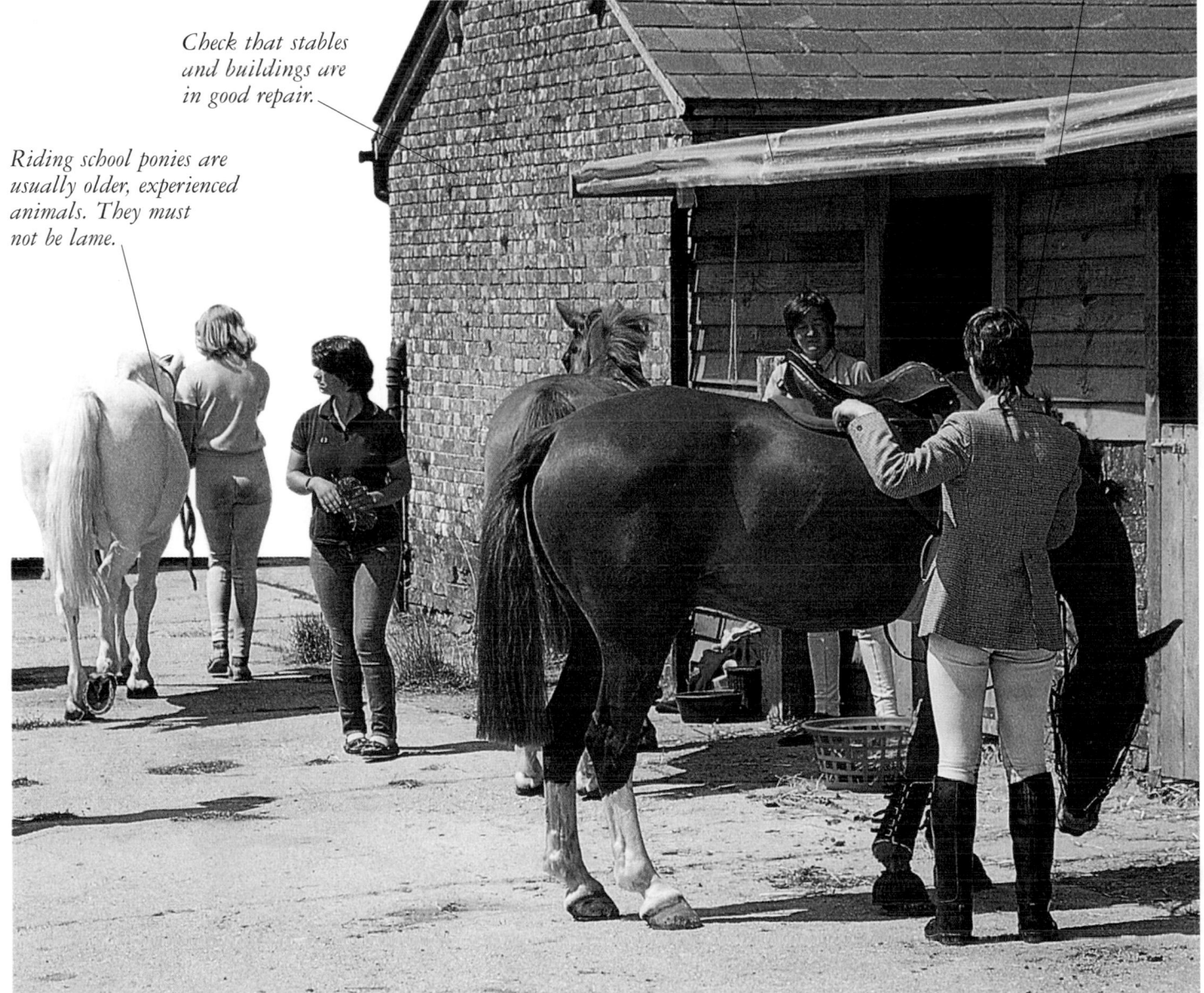

Ponies must have shelter from bad weather and shade from heat when tied up.

Instructor should check tack before rider mounts.

Check that stables and buildings are in good repair.

Riding school ponies are usually older, experienced animals. They must not be lame.

TACKING UP

TACK UP IN A STABLE, or outside with a headcollar fastened round the horse's neck so that you have control over it. Try to be gentle and quiet when you tack up, so that the horse remains calm. Make sure that the tack is safe and check it regularly for loose stitching or cracked leather.

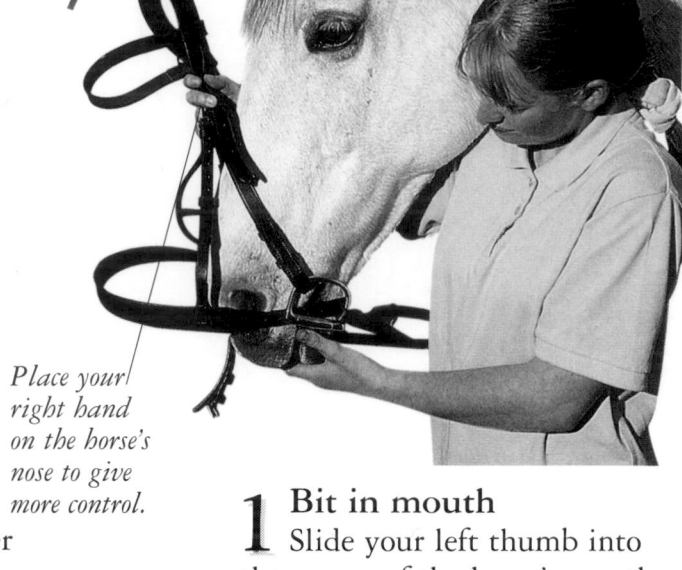

Place your right hand on the horse's nose to give more control.

Putting on a bridle

Before you start to put on a bridle, make sure the noseband and throatlatch are undone. Put the reins over the horse's head, remove the headcollar, and fasten it around the horse's neck to prevent it from walking away.

1 Bit in mouth
Slide your left thumb into the corner of the horse's mouth and gently guide the bit in.

Treat ears with care.

2 Over the ears
Put the headpiece over the horse's ears and place the ears through the gap between the headpiece and browband. Try not to pinch the ears. Take the forelock out from under the browband.

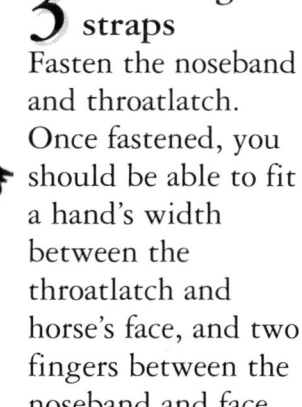

3 Fastening straps
Fasten the noseband and throatlatch. Once fastened, you should be able to fit a hand's width between the throatlatch and horse's face, and two fingers between the noseband and face.

Check that the bit fits comfortably. If it is too low in the mouth, it could hit against the horse's teeth.

When you have buckled up the throatlatch, check that it fits correctly.

Taking off a bridle

Before removing the bridle, make sure the horse is secure with a headcollar around its neck. Then unfasten the noseband and throatlatch, bring the reins to the poll and slide the bridle and reins forwards and off. Wait for the horse to release the bit from its mouth, or the bit may get caught or bang on its teeth.

Bring the reins to the poll.

Check that the noseband and throatlatch are undone.

Putting on a saddle

First check that the stirrup irons are run up, the numnah is in place, and the girth is folded over the saddle.

Girth folded over saddle.

1 In position
Lower the saddle gently over withers and slide back into position so coat hairs lie flat.

2 Fastening girth
Pull numnah up into the saddle. Carefully release girth so that it dangles down. Reach under the horse's belly for the girth, and fasten it. You should be able to slide your fingers between the girth and the horse.

Fasten one buckle at a time.

Taking off a saddle

Take off your saddle with as much care as you put it on. Once you remove the saddle, put it where it will not get damaged.

Place leathers between irons and saddle.

1 Run up stirrups
First run the stirrups up the leathers so they do not bang against the horse. Undo the girth.

2 Remove saddle
Place the girth over the saddle. The outside of the girth should be facing away from the saddle, so that any dried mud does not scratch it. Carefully lift off the saddle.

Lift saddle from horse's back.

Saddle must not pinch withers.

The stirrups should always be run up when you are not riding.

The girth should be tight enough to stop the saddle from sliding.

If leaving the horse tied up, twist reins under the throatlatch.

All tacked up

Once you have finished tacking up, check all fastenings and that the tack fits correctly. The bit should be high enough to fit snugly into the corners of the mouth. Straighten the bit, noseband, and browband if necessary. Tighten the girth, then gently pull each foreleg forwards to release any wrinkled skin.

WELL-FITTED SADDLE
A horse can only work well if its tack fits and is comfortable. The tree, or frame, of a saddle must be the correct width. A properly fitted saddle will not pinch, rub, or interfere with the horse's movement.

MOUNTING AND DISMOUNTING

ONE OF THE FIRST things you learn when you start riding is how to get on and off a pony. One way to mount is to put one foot in the stirrup and to spring up. You can also mount by standing on a mounting block, or by asking for a leg up. There are also different ways to dismount.

Mounting
Before you begin to mount, make sure the girth is tight enough to stop the saddle sliding around. Most riders mount from the left side, facing the pony's tail.

Landing heavily may cause the pony discomfort.

Leg clears pony's back

Keep reins short so that the pony does not move forwards.

Stand with your left shoulder next to the pony's left shoulder.

2 Lowering into saddle
Swing your right leg over the pony's back being careful not to kick the pony. Gently lower yourself into the saddle.

Sit straight in the saddle.

1 Foot in the stirrup
Turn the back edge of the stirrup iron towards you, place your left foot in and spring off your right foot.

3 In the saddle
Slip your right foot into the stirrup iron. Take up a light feel on the reins and sit up tall. Check your girth before you ride off.

Dismounting

Get off with as much care and consideration as you used to get on. You may need to ask someone to help if you are getting off a young or difficult pony.

Lean forwards to start the swing down.

Keep reins short so that you are in control of the pony.

Try to avoid kicking or prodding the pony as you dismount.

1 Start of dismount
Take both feet out of the stirrups, lean forwards and swing your right leg carefully over the pony's back.

Swing right leg over pony's back.

Bend your knees as you land on the ground.

2 Jumping down
Let yourself down in a quiet, smooth jump without pulling the saddle over. Try to keep your balance as you land.

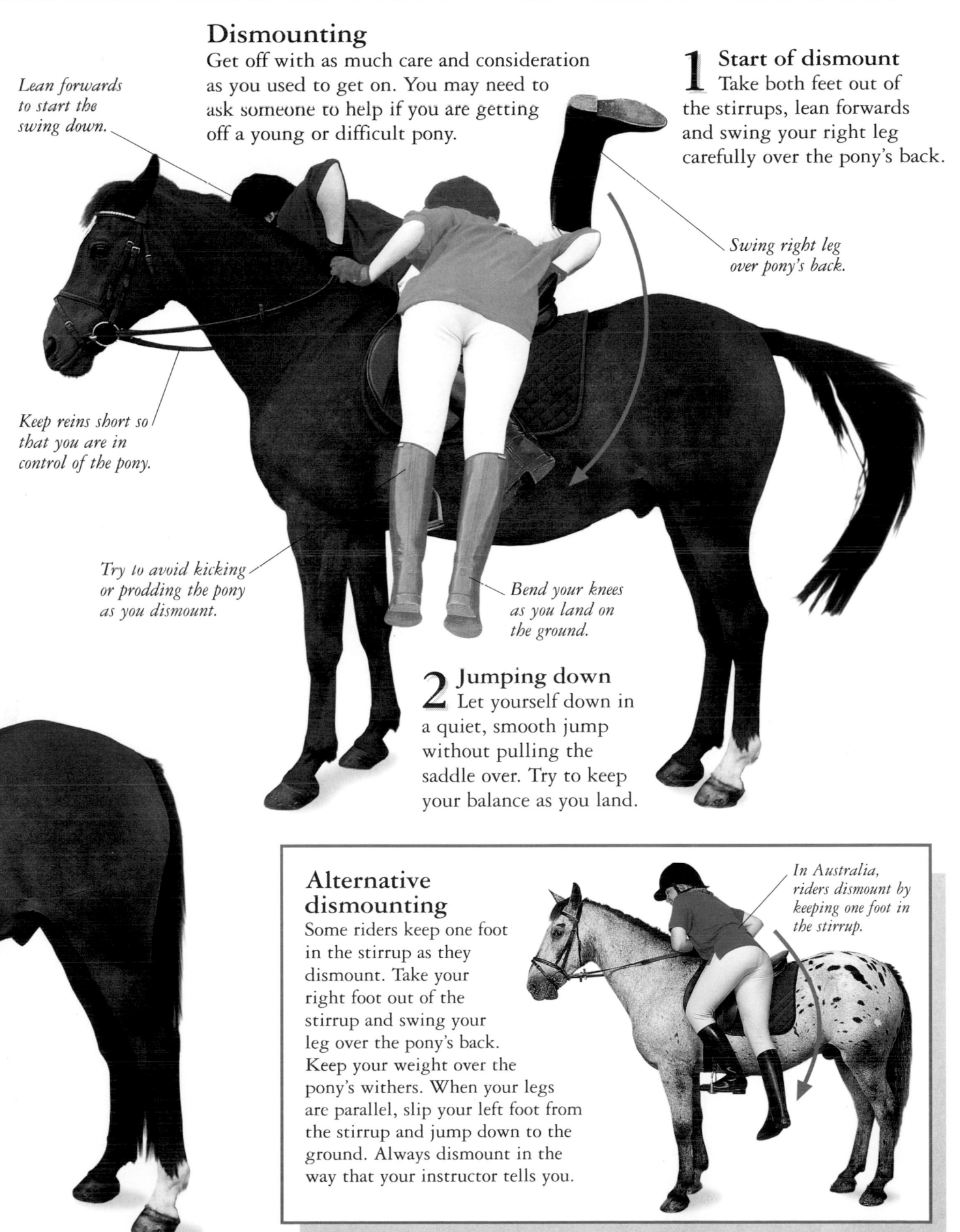

Alternative dismounting

Some riders keep one foot in the stirrup as they dismount. Take your right foot out of the stirrup and swing your leg over the pony's back. Keep your weight over the pony's withers. When your legs are parallel, slip your left foot from the stirrup and jump down to the ground. Always dismount in the way that your instructor tells you.

In Australia, riders dismount by keeping one foot in the stirrup.

IN THE SADDLE

LESSONS ON THE LUNGE or lead rein will get you used to the feel of sitting on a moving horse. Your instructor will help you achieve the correct position so that you and your horse are well balanced. You will also learn to give your horse clear instructions, called aids, with your legs, hands, and body weight. If you give the correct aids, and your horse is well trained, you will soon feel in control.

Hold the reins slightly apart, with your thumbs on top.

HOLDING THE REINS
Hold the reins in both hands, so that they pass between your little and fourth fingers, through your palms, and out between your first fingers and thumbs.

Your first lesson

Your first lesson is usually on the lunge and may be spent mainly at a walk, though you may be able to try a few trotting strides. Your instructor will control the horse, so you can concentrate on your riding technique. Do not worry if there seems to be a lot to remember – it becomes easier with practise.

Keep your arms relaxed.

Ask the horse to walk by squeezing its sides equally with both legs.

Contact with the horse's mouth should be light, not pulling back.

A horse on a lunge rein travels in a circle.

FIRST LESSON

- Feel the horse's mouth without pulling on the reins

- Look ahead, not down

- There should be a straight (perpendicular) line through your shoulder, elbow, hip, and heel

- Think about absorbing the horse's movements through your lower back

- Think about sitting tall but staying supple

- Stirrups should stay under the widest part of your foot

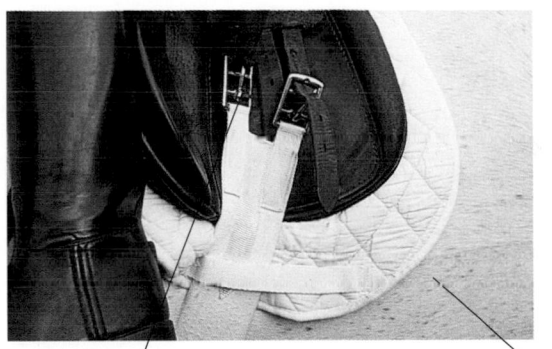

Adjust the buckles one at a time.

A horse may expand its belly as you tighten the girth, so check it again after a few minutes.

TIGHTENING THE GIRTH
During one of your first lessons, you may be taught how to tighten the girth. To do this, hold the reins in your right hand and swing your left leg forwards. Lift the saddle flap with your left hand and tighten the girth. You should be able to fit the flat of your fingers between the girth and the horse.

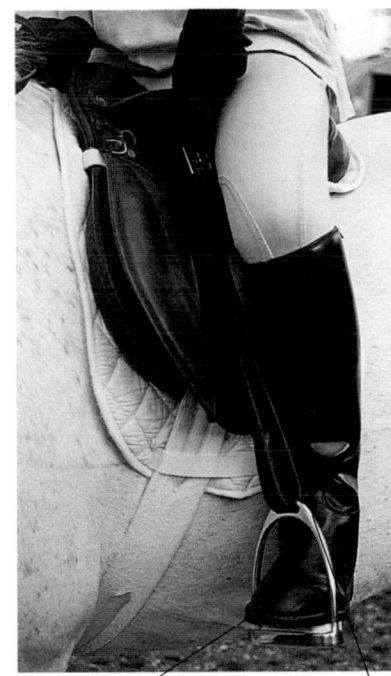

ADJUSTING STIRRUP LEATHERS
To adjust the stirrup leathers, hold the reins in one hand and pull the stirrup leather out and down, keeping your foot in the stirrup. Slide the buckle prong into the correct hole and pull the stirrup leather back up so the buckle is at the top again.

Markers are used for more complicated exercises in later lessons.

The manege, or riding arena, should be a safe, enclosed area.

Keep your toes pointing forwards and your heels down.

Keep your foot in the stirrup while you adjust the length of the stirrup leather.

The instructor controls your horse so you can concentrate on sitting correctly and getting used to the feel of a moving horse.

THE FIRST STEPS

WHEN YOU HAVE LEARNED how to sit on a horse in a walking gait, you will be ready to learn to control your horse's direction and speed by yourself. To communicate with a horse, give it signals with your legs, seat, hands, and voice. These are called the natural aids and will be used first of all to start, stop, and turn.

Voice

Hands

Sit tall, without bracing your back.

Seat

Reins should not be tight or hang in loops.

Legs

Starting off
Before moving off, check that your stirrups are the correct length and that your girth is tight enough. Your legs should rest lightly against the horse's sides and your reins should be at a length that gives a light contact with the horse's mouth, without pulling.

THE AIDS
The aids are signals that a horse is trained to understand. For example, a gentle squeeze of the legs means walk forwards, and closing the fingers on the reins means stop. Stop giving the aid as soon as the horse obeys, or it will become confused.

Straight line from elbows through hands to horse's mouth

Feel the side-to-side movement in the seat.

1 **Using the natural aids**
Look ahead and close both legs gently against the horse's sides. Stop squeezing as soon as it walks forwards. If there is no response, pause, then squeeze a little harder.

2 **Starting the walk**
Allow your hands to follow the movement of the horse's head, so contact with its mouth is light and flexible.

Walking gait

The walk has a 1-2-3-4 rhythm. The sequence of steps is left hind, left fore, right hind, and finally right fore. The horse always has at least two feet on the ground at any one time. A horse naturally has a long walk stride and a relaxed neck.

Right hindleg is followed by right foreleg.

Try not to restrict the walk when riding the horse.

Artificial aids

Experienced riders may use equipment such as whips, spurs, and martingales to give signals. These are called artificial aids and must be used with care. Whips and spurs must never be used to hurt a horse and should not be used by beginners.

Martingale helps control head carriage.

Schooling whip reinforces leg aids.

Spurs must be blunt.

Sitting tall and still helps to slow down horse.

Ears back and relaxed means horse is paying attention to rider.

Horse should stay relaxed through neck and mouth.

Outside leg is behind the girth to stop horse's hindquarters from swinging out.

Wrists should be supple and straight.

3 **To stop the horse**
To halt, sit tall and tighten your seat and thigh muscles. Close your fingers on the reins without pulling back. Keep your legs in contact with the horse's sides to keep the horse balanced.

Halt should be square with legs together.

Turning

When turning, look where you want to go, so that you position your weight correctly. To turn left, squeeze gently on the left rein and also with the left leg. Allow the right rein to slacken slightly so the horse's head can turn. Don't try to turn sharply.

TROTTING

A HORSE HAS FOUR GAITS – walk, trot, canter, and gallop – and you will learn about each in turn. Trot can be ridden sitting, when the movement is absorbed through the rider's lower back, or rising, when the rider sits and rises in time with the horse's stride. Both become easier with practise.

Start by riding on the right diagonal.

Sit for one beat then rise again to change diagonals.

Left hindfoot and right forefoot touch down together.

Learning to trot

Most riders spend more time in rising trot than in sitting trot. This is because as long as the rider is balanced and does not bump up and down, rising is more comfortable for the horse and easier for the rider. Western riders sit to a slow trot, called a jog.

DIAGONALS
Changing diagonals switches the position of the rider's weight. This makes riding easier for the horse, just like switching a heavy object from hand to hand makes it easier for you to carry. To change diagonals, sit for one beat, then rise again.

1 Moving forwards
To move forwards from a walk to a rising trot, close your legs against the horse's side in a quick inwards squeeze. Hold the reins to allow a light contact with the horse's mouth.

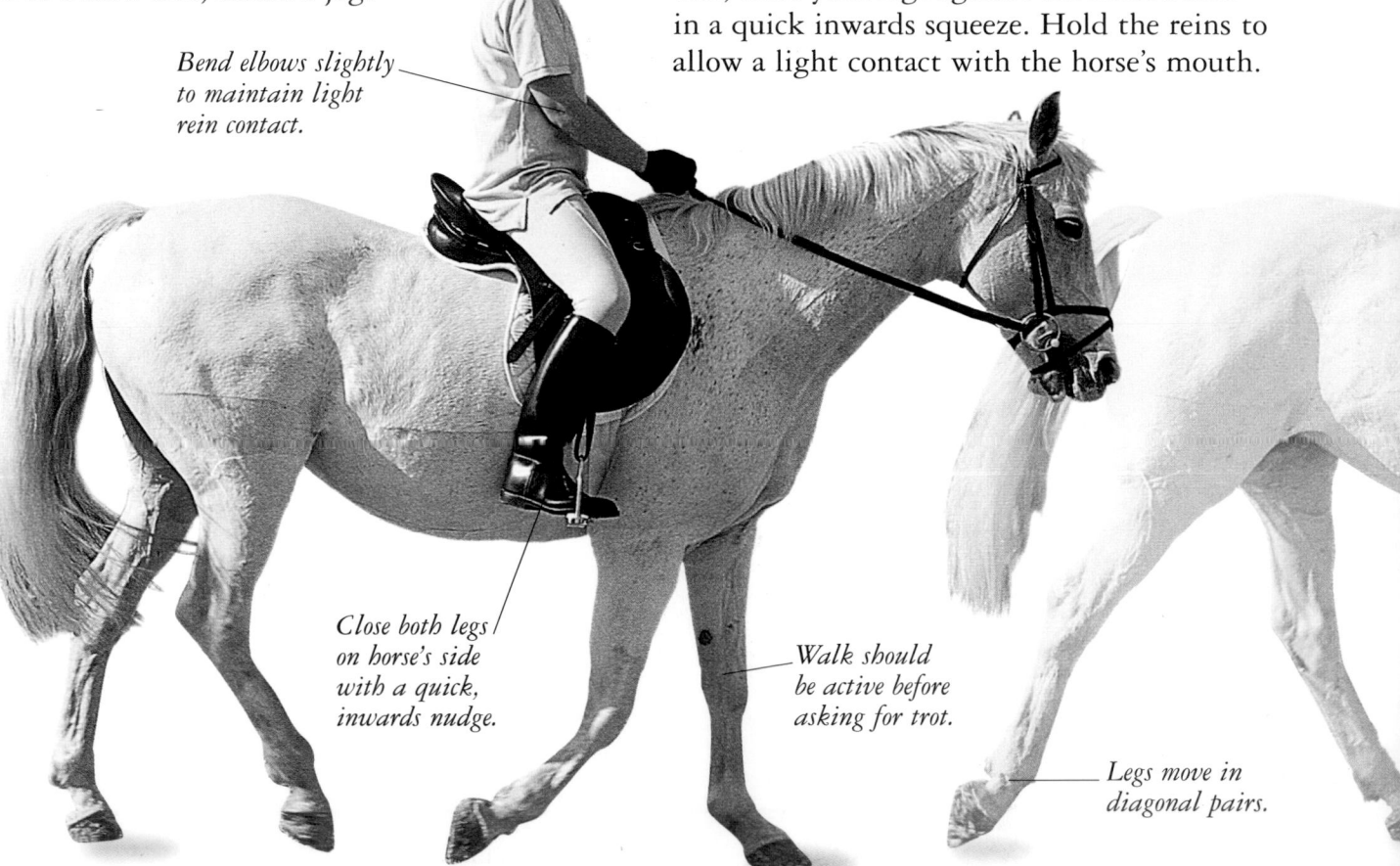

Bend elbows slightly to maintain light rein contact.

Close both legs on horse's side with a quick, inwards nudge.

Walk should be active before asking for trot.

Legs move in diagonal pairs.

Trotting gait

The trot is a two-time gait in which the legs move in diagonal pairs. The right (offside) foreleg and left (nearside) hindleg move forwards at the same time in a 1-2, 1-2 rhythm. A trotting horse naturally moves in balance, with rhythmic strides.

Only one foreleg or hindleg bears the horse's weight at any one time.

Hock joints provide power to push horse forwards.

Rise in a slightly forwards, not upwards, position.

2 Rising up into trot
Let the horse's stride push you slightly forwards and out of the saddle. Do not grip with your knees or try to stand in the stirrups.

Horse's movement pushes you out of the saddle.

Move back into saddle as gently as possible.

3 Sitting down
Sink back into the saddle and let the horse's movement push you forwards and out again. Counting the 1-2, 1-2 rhythm of the trot out loud might help.

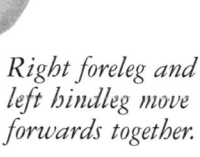
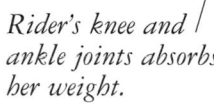

Right foreleg and left hindleg move forwards together.

Rider's knee and ankle joints absorbs her weight.

EXERCISES IN THE SADDLE

EXERCISES IN AND OUT of the saddle will help you become confident and supple when riding. It is important that the horse on which you practise mounted exercises is quiet and safe, and that your instructor is in control. Riding without stirrups will improve your balance and can be done on or off the lunge. Ride without stirrups only in safe surroundings – not on the roads. The more relaxed and confident you become, the more your horse will trust you and your riding will improve.

This exercise improves your agility and tones your thigh and stomach muscles.

Swing right leg over withers, taking care not to touch the horse.

Instructor holds horse so that it remains still during the exercise.

Round-the-world

Before starting this exercise, remove the stirrups or cross them in front of the saddle so that they are out of the way. This exercise is easier to perform in an anticlockwise direction. Swing your right leg over the horse's withers to sit sideways, then swing your left leg over the quarters to face the tail. Continue until you are facing forwards again.

Keep your leg stretched downwards as you swing the other leg over the withers or hindquarters.

Without stirrups

Riding without stirrups is an excellent way to improve your balance and helps you absorb the horse's movement through your lower back. This exercise is especially good for improving your sitting trot. Start off by riding without stirrups for short periods, then rest.

Side reins control horse's head carriage when it is on the lunge.

Allow your legs to stretch down without gripping with your knees.

Forward stretch

This exercise helps you improve your balance. While walking, bend forwards from the hip and stretch out your arms towards the horse's ears. Try to keep your lower leg in the correct position, without moving it too far forwards or back.

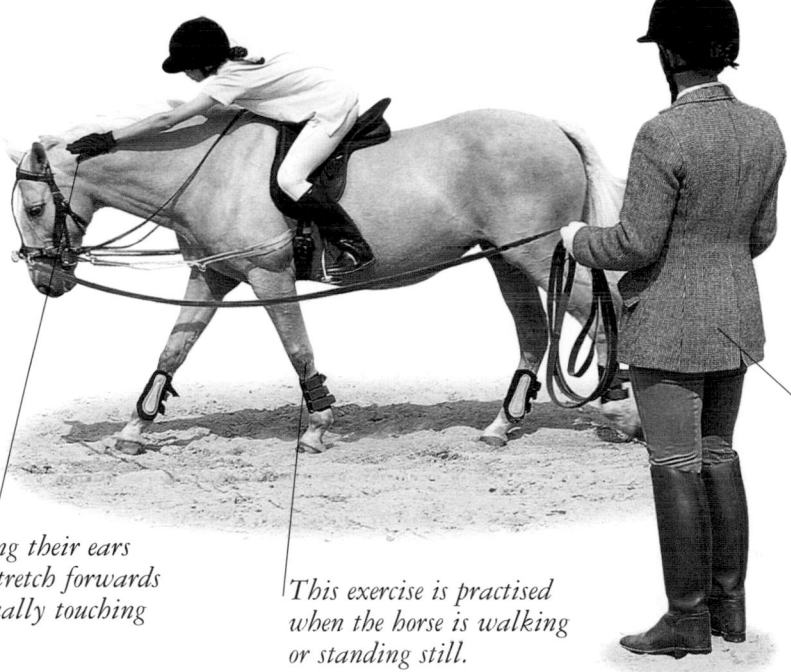

A moving horse must be controlled by an instructor.

Some horses dislike having their ears touched, so stretch forwards without actually touching the horse.

This exercise is practised when the horse is walking or standing still.

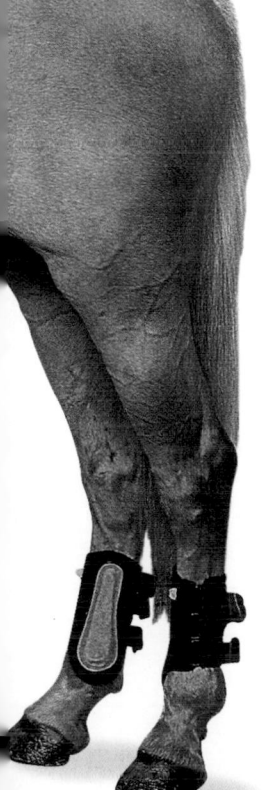

Keeping fit

There are lots of ways to improve your fitness and suppleness, even when you are unable to ride. Swimming is excellent for all-over exercise and uses many of the muscles you use when riding. Cycling and skipping are also beneficial for building leg muscles. Increase exercise times gradually or you may end up with aching muscles! Floor exercises such as the ones shown here may also help.

Swing each leg forwards and backwards from the hip to loosen muscles.

Jump up into the air and stretch upwards as far as you can.

Start off in a squatting position with your hands at your sides.

CANTERING AND GALLOPING

THE CANTER AND THE GALLOP are faster than the trot. The gallop is the fastest gait of all and when galloping you must stay in complete control. During a gallop, bend forwards from the hips so that your weight is just out of the saddle and is absorbed by your knees and ankles. During a canter, sit upright but remain relaxed, and absorb the horse's movement through your lower back.

Sit upright, but remain relaxed and look ahead.

Horse takes a longer stride with its right leg.

THE LEADING LEG
A cantering horse takes a longer stride with one foreleg than the other. This is called the leading leg. On a circle or bend, the correct leading leg is the inside leg – for example, in a clockwise circle, the right leg leads.

Preparing to canter
Before you ask a horse to canter, establish a balanced but active trot. It is easier to get the correct leading leg (also called the correct strike-off) by asking for a canter when you are trotting in a circle or in one corner of the arena.

1 Ask for canter
Maintain an active trot without rushing. Sit for one or two strides, then brush your outside leg slightly behind the horse's girth. At the same time nudge your inside leg near the horse's girth.

2 The canter
Try not to restrict the horse's head and neck as it moves into the canter. Sit tall but remain relaxed, and keep your lower back supple to absorb the movement.

Keep contact with the horse's mouth.

Trot should be active before you "ask for canter".

Galloping

Once you can canter properly, you can learn to gallop. Instead of sitting as you do for a canter, bend forwards from the hips and shift your weight just out of the saddle. Only gallop in safe surroundings where the visibility and terrain are good. You should be in control of the pace, not the horse. The gallop has a 1,2,3,4 four-beat gait.

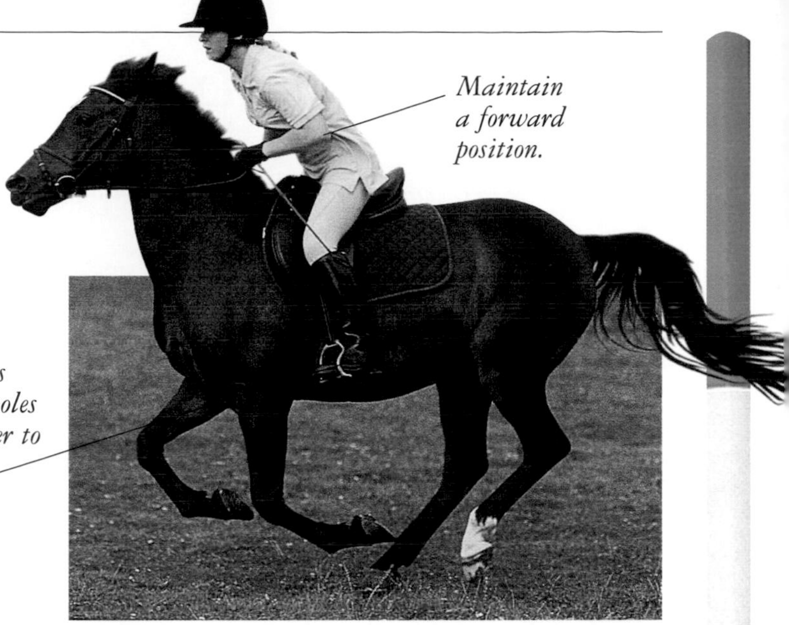

Maintain a forward position.

Shorten stirrups by one or two holes to make it easier to stay balanced.

Cantering gait

A canter has a 1,2,3 three-beat gait. When the horse's right leg leads, the left hindfoot falls first, then the right hindfoot and the left forefoot together, then the right forefoot.

Hindquarters provide power.

Horse's neck stretches as speed increases.

Use your weight distribution and the rein to give the horse a "slow down" signal.

3 Slowing down
To return to a trot, sit up and tighten your thigh and seat muscles. At the same time, close your fingers on the reins without pulling back.

4 Back to a trot
As the horse moves into a trot, relax your fingers on the reins. Sit for one stride, then move forwards into a rising trot.

Changing pace is called making a transition.

A trot is often more energetic just after the horse has cantered.

MAKING PROGRESS

YOUR FIRST LESSONS will be given to you on your own by an instructor, but as you gain confidence you will probably join a group lesson with other new riders. During the group lessons you will learn how to control your horse around other horses, and how to perform different exercises in the manege (riding arena). You will develop your knowledge of aids so that you can communicate more effectively with your horse.

Left rein instructs the horse which direction to follow.

Right rein allows the horse to turn.

Using the correct aids
Your instructor will help you to develop a more detailed knowledge of how to use the aids. For example, to turn left, look left, squeeze the left rein, and release the right rein slightly. At the same time, close your left leg on the horse's side and move your right leg back to control the angle of the hindquarters.

Group lessons
Your group will contain up to five or six riders. Riding in a group teaches you to be more aware of other horses and their riders. Always keep a safe distance from the horse in front, since it might kick.

The first rider is called the leading file.

Make sure you do not bump into the horse in front.

Passing side by side

When you pass another horse and rider, you need to make sure that you do not bump into them. The easiest way to do this is to pass so that your left hand is next to the other rider's left hand. This is called riding left hand to left hand.

Left hands are next to each other as you pass.

When passing a horse that you do not know, or that is unpredictable, allow enough space in case it kicks.

THE MANEGE

Manege comes from the French word for "horsemanship". Letters placed around the outside of the arena are used as guides for starting and finishing circles and other exercises called school figures. A standard arena is 20 m x 40 m (65$^1/_2$ ft x 131 ft).

SCHOOL FIGURES

THE STANDARD ARENA

This standard arena is ideal for school exercises.

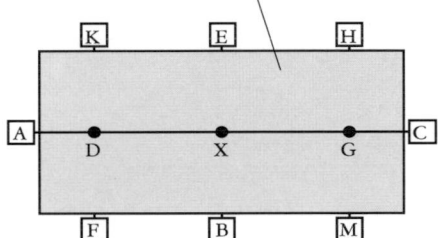

The letters around the arena are always A, K, E, H, C, M, B, and F. Markers D, X, and G are placed along the centre of the arena.

CIRCLES

The small circle is 10 m (33 ft) in diameter.

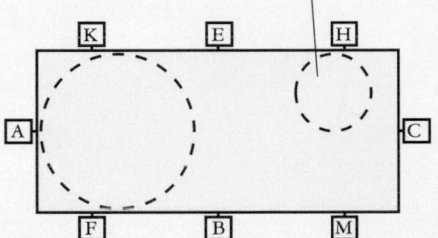

You can ride 20-m (66-ft) circles in a walk, trot, and canter from A, C, B, or E. Advanced horses and riders ride in smaller circles.

CHANGING THE REIN

The figure of eight enables you to change direction.

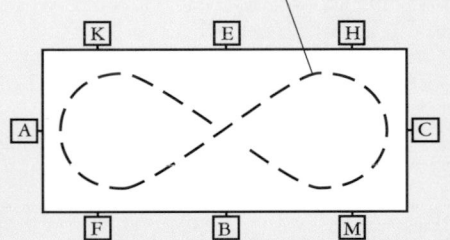

Turning across the arena to change direction is called changing the rein. In this case it is practised across the diagonal.

Slow down in plenty of time.

All riders in a group should have similar experience.

LEARNING TO JUMP

ONCE YOU CAN TROT and canter confidently, you can learn to jump. Before you start, you need to shorten your stirrups two or three holes so that you can stay in balance and follow your horse's movement. Always warm up before jumping so your horse is supple and obedient.

Ground pole is at correct distance from fence for horse's stride length.

FIRST JUMP
Your first jump will be two poles in a low cross, approached from trot. A correctly placed pole on the ground in front, called a ground pole, helps you arrive at the correct take-off point.

How a horse jumps

There are five phases to a jump – the approach, take-off, (suspension) in the air, landing, and getaway. Keep your approach positive but calm, whether you are riding in trot or canter, and meet the fence straight. Look ahead and let your weight sink down to your heels.

Knees act as shock absorbers.

Body weight should sink down through your legs into your heels.

1 Take off
As the horse takes off, fold your upper body forwards from the hips, and slide your hands far enough up the horse's neck to allow it freedom to stretch.

Rider allows horse freedom of head and neck.

Horse pushes off with both back feet.

Trotting poles encourage horse to flex hocks.

2 In the air
Think about sliding your seat backwards as you fold; do not stand up in the stirrups. As the horse's head and neck stretch forwards and down, give slightly with the reins.

TROTTING POLES
Poles spaced to allow one or more trot strides between them are called trotting poles. Use these to practise establishing a rhythmic stride and to introduce inexperienced horses to coloured poles.

JUMPING PROBLEMS

If you are having problems, keep calm and go back to basics: perhaps your approach was hesitant or too fast. Never jump without a knowledgeable helper to advise you and alter fences. Always be ready to lower fences to make things easier and to restore the confidence of both you and your horse.

REFUSAL

A horse may stop in front of a fence or duck out to the side. This is called a refusal. A horse may refuse if the fence is too large or difficult – if so adjust the fence. Make your second approach straight, riding positively but not fast. You may have more control approaching in trot.

CAT JUMP

A horse that jumps awkwardly instead of following a smooth arc (bascule) through the air is said to cat jump. It usually happens when the horse takes off too close to the fence or is hesitant. To avoid this, try to establish a rhythm to the horse's strides and be positive.

Upper body becomes more upright.

Look up and ahead, either to your next fence or straight ahead if jumping a single fence.

Stirrup under widest part of foot

Light, unrestricting rein contact

3 Landing

As the horse lands, allow your upper body to become upright, without leaning back. Absorb landing impact through knees and ankles.

Horses should always wear protective boots.

Falling off

Everyone falls off occasionally, often because the horse or rider loses balance. Minimize the impact of falling by always wearing a hard hat or helmet and body protector. If you do fall, don't keep hold of the reins since the horse may step on you.

HACKING OUT

RIDING IN THE OPEN is called hacking out and is lots of fun. Horses enjoy hacks and may be livelier than usual, so your instructor will make sure you are a confident and competent rider before taking you out. Most hacks last for about one or two hours and consist of a group of horses and riders. Before going on your first hack, make sure you know the rules of road safety, and that you have the right equipment.

Be aware of your horse's nature.

HACKING HAZARDS
During a hack, you may have to cope with potential hazards, such as riding through water. If your horse is reluctant or nervous, keep calm and allow a confident horse and rider to go first. This is called giving a lead, and gives an inexperienced horse confidence.

Out and about
Before you leave the riding school, always tell someone where you are going and when you expect to be back. When out, respect rights-of-way and ride slowly past farm animals and people. Canter only when the ground is suitable and when you can see far enough ahead.

The most experienced rider should set a pace that everyone can keep up with.

Check the girth before riding out.

HACKING OUT SAFELY

The correct preparations and equipment will enable you to hack out in safety and with enjoyment. Only experienced horses should be taken out alone. Never hack out on a horse that is nervous in traffic, and ride out only when you are feeling confident.

CHECKING BEFORE RIDE

CHECK TACK
Before you set out, it is important to check that your tack is in good condition and correctly fitted to the horse. Make sure that your girth is tight enough and that all straps are fastened properly, with any loose ends pushed through the securing loops. There should be no wrinkles or folds in pads or cloths used underneath the saddle.

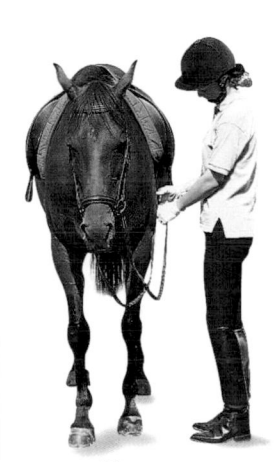

TACKING UP

CHECK SHOES
Pick out the horse's feet with a hoofpick and be sure all four shoes are in good condition. If a shoe is loose, the horse should not be ridden until the farrier has replaced it.

SAFETY EQUIPMENT

FLUORESCENT CLOTHING
Wearing fluorescent, reflective clothing in dull weather makes you more visible to other road users, especially drivers. Safety equipment includes belts and tabards for riders, leg bands for horses, and lights that clip onto the stirrup irons.

SAFETY KIT

Fit leg bands on to horse.

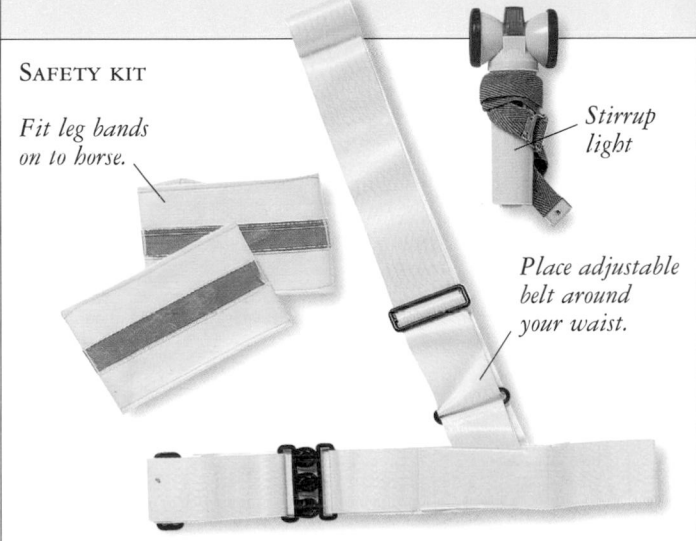

Stirrup light

Place adjustable belt around your waist.

ROAD SAFETY

OBSERVATION
To hack out safely, be observant. Look ahead and behind before you move off, change direction, or pull out to move around parked cars or other hazards. If you come to a road junction, stop and look in all directions, making sure it is safe before you proceed. Look ahead for things that may make your horse shy, such as roadworks, then check the road is free from traffic before riding past these obstacles. Never rely on your hearing – some cars are quiet and bicycles can't be heard. Keep to the side of the road, so other road users can pass.

Remember to check behind as well as in front.

ROAD SENSE

HAND SIGNALS
Give hand signals before crossing roads or turning out of junctions and look both ahead and behind to make sure the road is clear before moving off. To turn right, hold your reins in your left hand and extend your right arm. To turn left, put the reins in your right hand and extend your left arm. Use the hand signals early enough and always ride on the same side as the traffic. Like motorists and cyclists, you must obey all road signs and traffic lights. Not all road users realize they can frighten a horse and will not warn you if they are near. Always thank drivers who slow down or wait.

Always look and signal before turning.

RIDING MANNERS

ADVANCED RIDING

WHEN YOU CAN RIDE confidently at all paces, you can learn more advanced movements. Your horse must already be trained to do these exercises, or it will not understand your aids. All the exercises shown here help to make a horse more supple and balanced. They are useful for all forms of riding, as well as dressage.

HOW A HORSE TURNS ON THE FOREHAND
As the horse looks to the right, the right hindleg crosses in front of the left one. At the same time, the horse pivots on its right foreleg. The horse should not move forwards or backwards.

Turning on the spot

This exercise is useful when opening gates. It is also the first step in teaching a horse to move sideways. When the horse moves its hindquarters around its front end, it is called a turn on the forehand. At first, ask for just a few steps.

2 Move sideways
Hold your left leg on the girth and feel gently on the left rein to ask the horse to move sideways, not forwards or backwards.

Rider must sit straight and must not pull back on the reins.

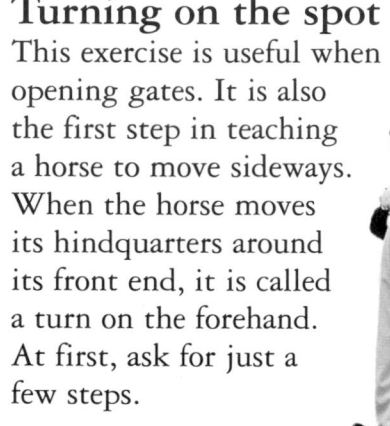

1 Begin turn
To turn to the right, squeeze your fingers on the right rein and put your right leg back to nudge the horse behind the girth.

Right hindleg crosses over in front of left.

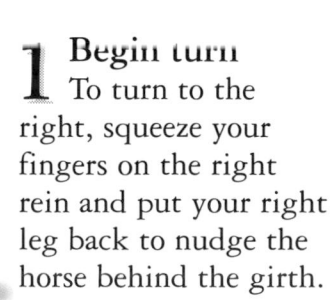

Don't practise this exercise too often or for too long.

3 Using legs
Use your right leg in time with the horse's steps, not as a constant push. Practise this exercise in both directions by using the opposite rein and leg aids.

Rein back

When your horse can rein back, it is easier for you to open gates and manoeuvre in tight spaces. You will need to start this exercise from halt. Close both legs behind the girth; at the same time, close your fingers on the reins and sit lightly to tell the horse to step backwards, not forwards. You can teach a horse to rein back by asking a helper to press gently on its chest as you give the aids.

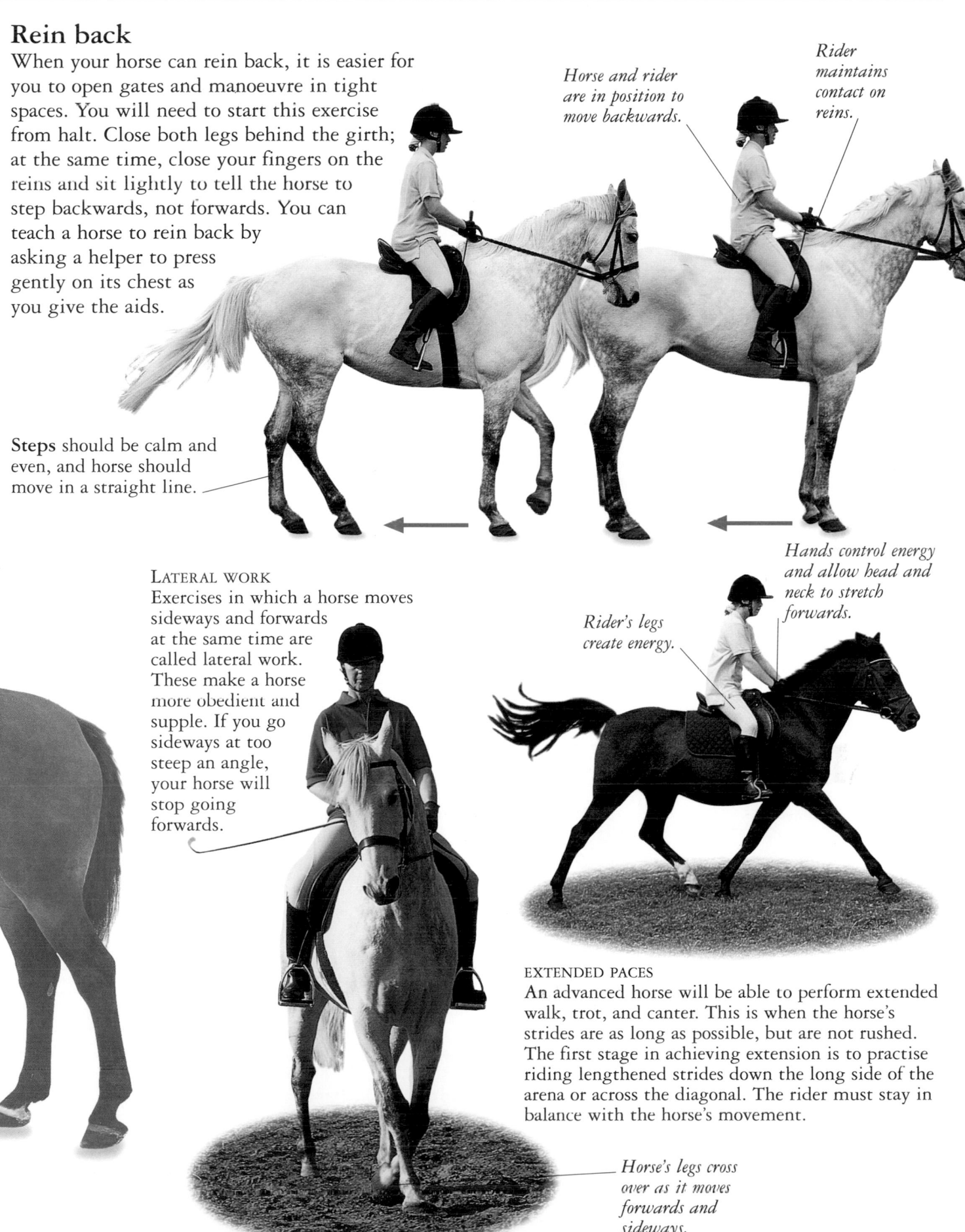

Horse and rider are in position to move backwards.

Rider maintains contact on reins.

Steps should be calm and even, and horse should move in a straight line.

LATERAL WORK

Exercises in which a horse moves sideways and forwards at the same time are called lateral work. These make a horse more obedient and supple. If you go sideways at too steep an angle, your horse will stop going forwards.

Rider's legs create energy.

Hands control energy and allow head and neck to stretch forwards.

EXTENDED PACES

An advanced horse will be able to perform extended walk, trot, and canter. This is when the horse's strides are as long as possible, but are not rushed. The first stage in achieving extension is to practise riding lengthened strides down the long side of the arena or across the diagonal. The rider must stay in balance with the horse's movement.

Horse's legs cross over as it moves forwards and sideways.

ADVANCED JUMPING

ONCE YOU HAVE MASTERED the basics of jumping, you can enjoy challenges such as jumping courses and tackling cross-country fences. To improve your technique, your instructor will set up jumping exercises in which a certain number of strides are allowed between each fence. This is called gridwork. Practice fences should be small. Never jump without having someone there to help.

CROSS-COUNTRY
Cross-country courses are ridden at a faster canter than showjumping ones and are set over distances of about 1.6–4.8 km (1–3 miles). Some fences, such as drop fences and some water jumps, should be approached at a trot.

Jumping a course
A novice showjumping course has about 10 fences. Approach each fence straight on at an energetic but controlled pace, and make sure your horse always canters on the correct leg. If necessary, jump from a trot.

Look up and ahead, not down at the fence.

Allow the horse to stretch its head and neck forwards as it jumps.

Protective boots should be put on a horse when jumping to minimize the risk of injury.

WARMING UP
Warm up over a single fence before jumping a whole course. Start with a cross pole, which is easy for the horse.

Gridwork

A grid is a row of fences that are spaced at set distances to allow the horse to take a certain number of strides between them. It helps train the horse into meeting each fence correctly so that you can concentrate on riding correctly. More difficult grids improve a horse's athletic ability. Always get help to adjust the fences.

Distances are set according to the length of your horse's stride.

Bounce jumps

Bounce fences make you and your horse more athletic. They are set so that the horse lands after the first jump and then immediately jumps over the second without taking any strides in between.

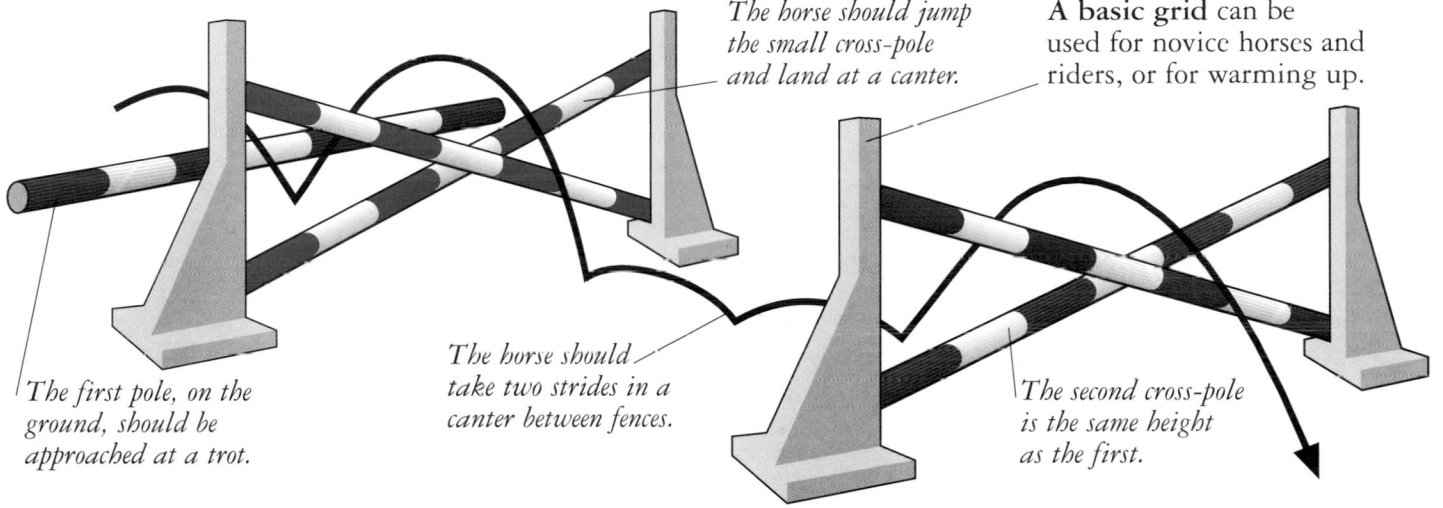

The horse should jump the small cross-pole and land at a canter.

A basic grid can be used for novice horses and riders, or for warming up.

The first pole, on the ground, should be approached at a trot.

The horse should take two strides in a canter between fences.

The second cross-pole is the same height as the first.

JUMPING DISTANCES

Distances between the two fences of a double are set according to a horse's size and stride length, and the type of jump used. The higher and wider the jump, the more room is needed. This chart shows some distances used between upright and parallel fences.

ONE NON-JUMPING STRIDE

HORSE HEIGHTS	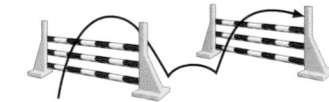		
	TWO UPRIGHT FENCES	AN UPRIGHT THEN PARALLEL	TWO PARALLELS
Over 14.2 hh	7.30m–7.90m (24ft–26ft)	7.15m–7.60m (23ft 6in–25ft)	7m–7.30m (23ft–24ft)
14.2 hh	6.55m–7.45m (21ft 6in–24ft 6in)	6.55m–7.15m (21ft 6in–23ft 6in)	Not used
13.2 hh	6.25m–7m (20ft 6in–23ft)	Not used	Not used

TWO NON-JUMPING STRIDES

HORSE HEIGHTS			
	TWO UPRIGHT FENCES	AN UPRIGHT THEN PARALLEL	TWO PARALLELS
Over 14.2 hh	10.50m–10.95m (34ft 6in–36ft)	10.50m–10.80m (34ft 6in–35ft 6in)	10.35m–10.65m (34ft–35ft)
14.2 hh	9.60m–10.65m (31ft 6in–35ft)	9.60m–10.20m (31ft 6in–33ft 6in)	9.60m–10.20m (31ft 6in–33ft 6in)
13.2 hh	9.15m–10.20m (30ft–33ft 6in)	9.15m–9.90m (30ft–32ft 6in)	9.15m–9.90m (30ft–32ft 6in)

WESTERN RIDING

RIDING WESTERN STYLE, for pleasure and competition, is popular throughout the world. Western riders usually prefer to use curb bits or bitless bridles called hackamores. The reins are held loosely in one hand and the rider steers by leaning the rein against the horse's neck. This is called neck reining.

This rider is wearing casual Western clothes; show clothes have elaborate details.

Saddling up

Western riding equipment is different from English-style tack. The bridle has no noseband and it usually has a curb bit and split reins. The saddle has a high front and back, and the girth is called a cinch.

The saddle blanket is made from heavy wool.

1 Put on bridle
Hold the bridle in front of the horse's face and slip the bit into its mouth. The split headstall (the top) goes around either side of the horse's ears.

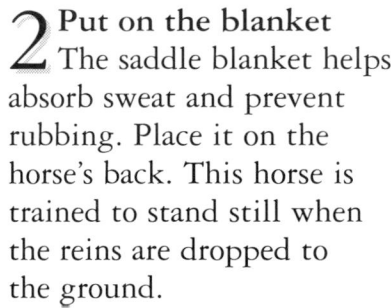

2 Put on the blanket
The saddle blanket helps absorb sweat and prevent rubbing. Place it on the horse's back. This horse is trained to stand still when the reins are dropped to the ground.

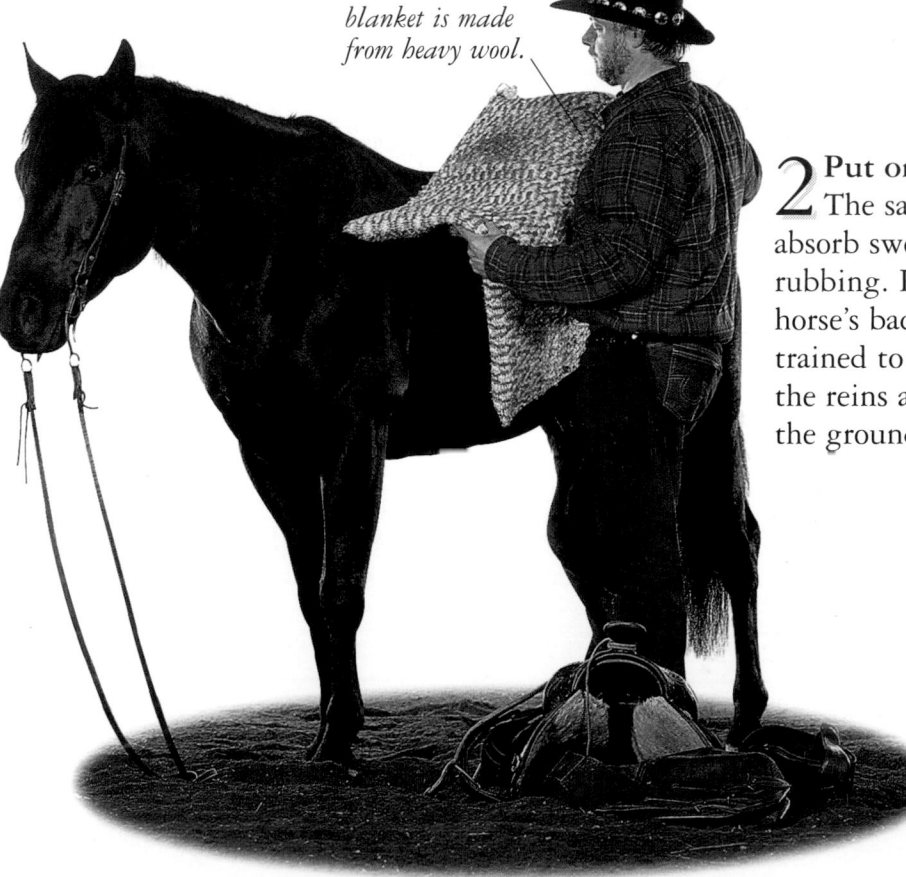

3 Put on the saddle
Position the saddle on the horse's back, move the left stirrup out of the way, then tighten the latigo (front) and cinch (girth) straps.

Western training

A highly trained Western horse will turn on the spot, move sideways, or make a sliding stop from a flat-out gallop in response to light aids. A horse can be trained so that it may be ridden in both English and Western styles.

OTHER RIDING STYLES
Riders of the Camargue, in France, ride in a style similar to that of Western riders and use similar saddles. They are called gardiens, and ride white Camargue stallions to herd the region's wild black bulls. Like Western horses, these horses are also trained to change direction quickly.

The ficheroun is a three-pronged pole used to control bulls.

Crupper helps keep saddle in place.

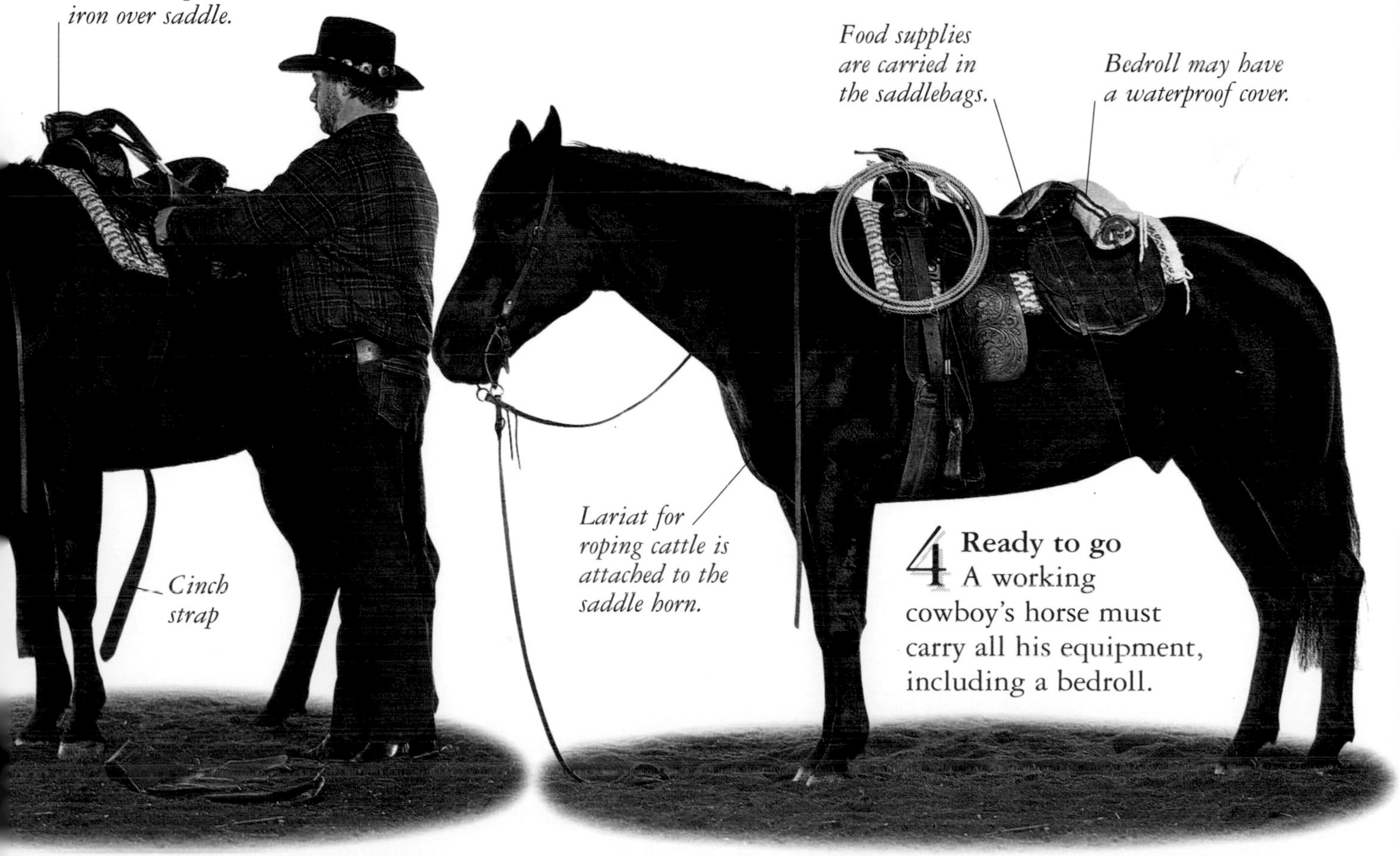

Place stirrup iron over saddle.

Cinch strap

Lariat for roping cattle is attached to the saddle horn.

Food supplies are carried in the saddlebags.

Bedroll may have a waterproof cover.

4 Ready to go
A working cowboy's horse must carry all his equipment, including a bedroll.

HELPING TO SCHOOL A HORSE

AN EXPERIENCED RIDER may be able to help school young or inexperienced horses. Schooling is enjoyable and rewarding, but must always be supervised by an expert. Practise skills such as long reining with an older, experienced horse before helping to teach a young one. Also, hack out a young horse in the company of a sensible horse and rider to boost the youngster's confidence before going out alone.

SCHOOLING A HORSE

- All training must be carried out under expert supervision

- Never push the horse too hard during its training

- Keep lessons short and finish on a positive note

- Riders and handlers should be dressed safely, and horses should wear protective boots

- Be confident about using long reins before starting to train a young or inexperienced horse

Early lessons

Lungeing and long reining teach a horse to obey voice commands. Long reining, where the trainer is positioned behind the horse, teaches it to stop, start, and turn and to accept the feel of a bit. This means that when a rider mounts the horse for the first time, the horse already understands some of the basic aids. Start by long reining in a safe, enclosed area.

Gloves prevent injury if the reins are pulled through your hands.

USING LONG REINS
Long reins may frighten a horse when used for the first time. Before going outside, introduce the reins in the stable so that the horse is used to feeling them around its legs. When using the long reins, remember to use voice commands at the same time.

Long reins

Hard hat or helmet should always be worn when working young horses.

Riding boots are the safest footwear since they will not slip.

Coil the long reins safely out of the way.

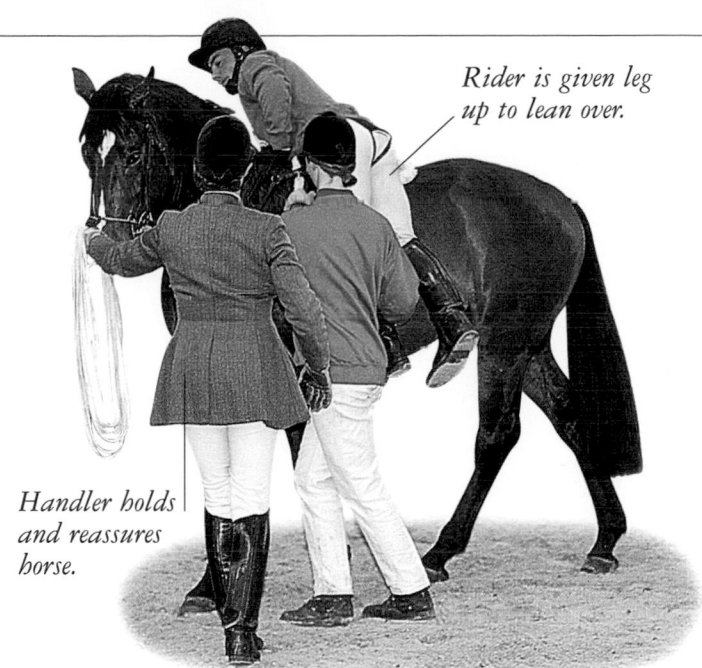

Rider is given leg up to lean over.

Handler holds and reassures horse.

Always wear a body protector.

BACKING A YOUNG HORSE

Teaching a horse to accept a rider is called backing. First the rider leans over the saddle so that the horse gets used to the weight. When the horse is comfortable with the weight, the rider places one foot in the stirrup and swings the other leg over the saddle. Riding horses should not be backed until they are three years old.

HELP FROM AN EXPERT

Introduce a horse to new skills, such as jumping, with expert help. An instructor will assess the horse's reaction to new experiences and judge when to progress to the next stage. Keep the first lessons short, and always finish on a good note so the horse stays relaxed.

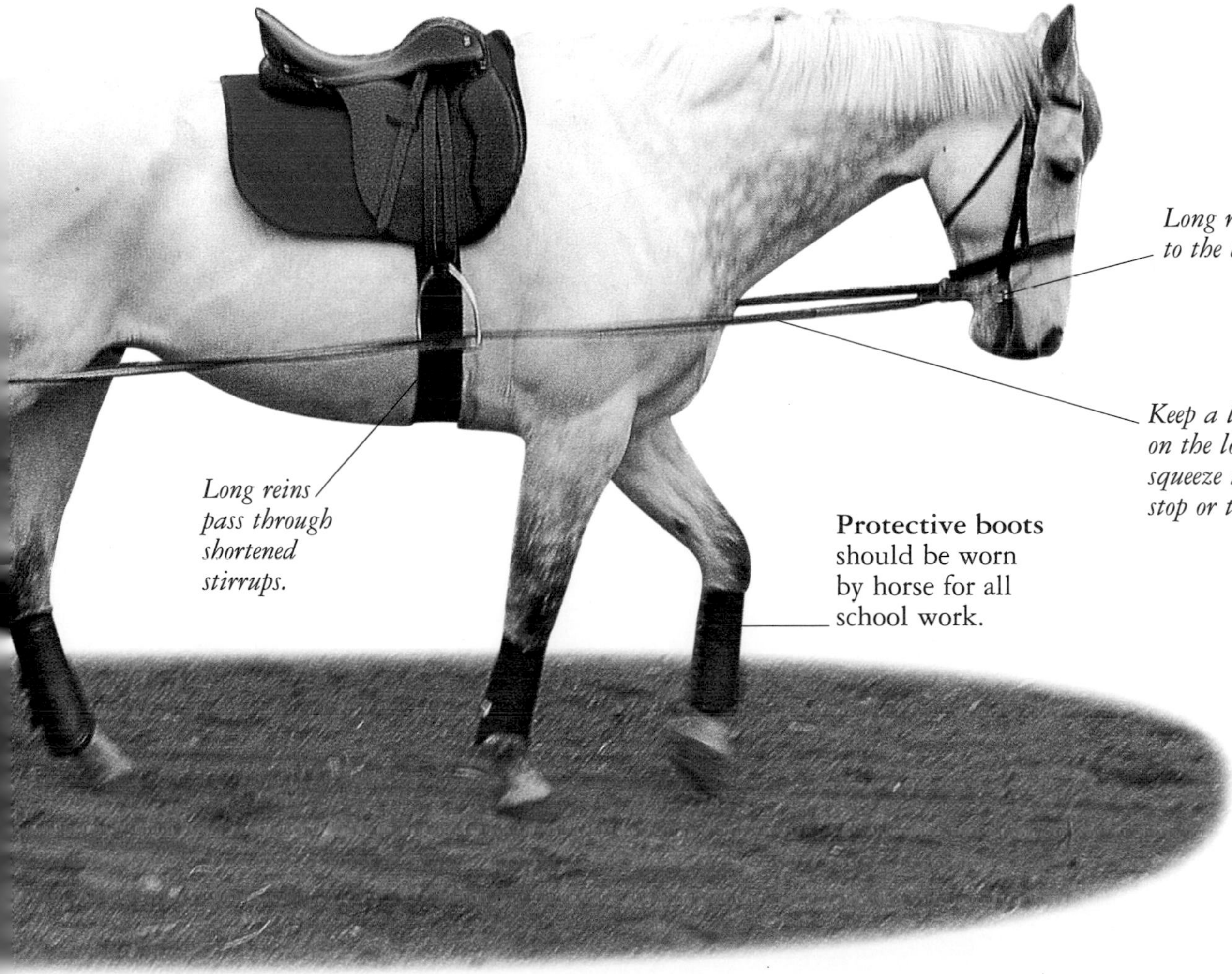

Long reins attach to the bit.

Keep a light hold on the long reins and squeeze them gently to stop or turn.

Long reins pass through shortened stirrups.

Protective boots should be worn by horse for all school work.

DIFFICULT PONIES

YOU MAY COME ACROSS PONIES that are difficult to ride or handle and that have specific behavioural problems. Never try to solve these problems alone – get help from an experienced adult. The expert should always start by checking that the pony is not uncomfortable or in pain, since this causes many problems. Ask your vet's advice if necessary, and get an expert to check the fit of your tack. Too much high-energy food and too little exercise will cause excitable or bad behaviour.

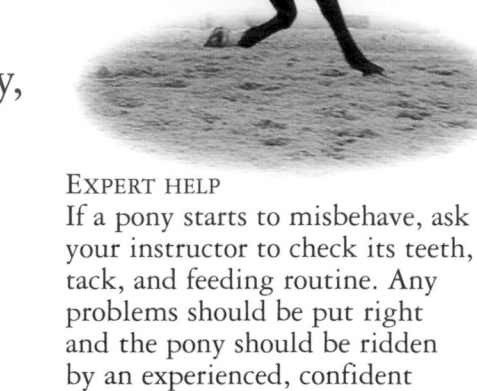

An experienced rider will not be thrown off the pony.

Check that saddle does not pinch.

EXPERT HELP
If a pony starts to misbehave, ask your instructor to check its teeth, tack, and feeding routine. Any problems should be put right and the pony should be ridden by an experienced, confident rider until it settles down.

Difficult temperaments

Healthy ponies that have been trained and handled correctly should be confident and friendly. Ponies that have had rushed or incorrect training sessions, or those that have had bad experiences, may be nervous or stubborn. Naturally aggressive ponies are rare, but some may bite or kick to prevent you from doing something they dislike.

Male horses and ponies, called stallions, may rear up onto their hind legs to fight, and they may use their teeth and forelegs.

When a pony's ears are laid back it is confused or frightened.

AGGRESSIVE PONIES
Horses and ponies are sometimes aggressive with each other, but rarely attack people. Some kick or bite if previous rough handling has caused them discomfort. Do not try to separate ponies that are fighting in the field since you may get hurt.

NERVOUS PONIES
A pony may be generally nervous, or worried about particular things, such as traffic. It must be handled in a quiet and confident manner and ridden by an expert. Never go for a hack on a traffic-shy pony. It must be re-schooled by an experienced professional.

COMMON PROBLEMS

All ponies misbehave occasionally and even the quietest ones may buck, rear, shy, or bolt if startled. Problems occur when bad behaviour becomes a habit. When a pony runs away out of control it is too dangerous for anyone but an expert to deal with.

RIDING PROBLEMS

BOLTING
A pony that bolts, runs off in a panic, and ignores its rider's signals to stop. Never ride a pony that is known to bolt. If a pony gallops off when you are already riding it, slow down by pulling and slackening the reins repeatedly; do not pull the reins continuously. Use your voice to reassure the pony.

SHYING
A shying pony may jump sideways if something frightens it. If you spot something that your pony might shy at, turn its head slightly away from the hazard, and look ahead as you ride past. Use your legs to keep a pony moving and try not to tense up since the pony will sense that you are nervous.

A REARING PONY

The pony must learn that it cannot get its own way by rearing.

REARING
If a pony rears while you are riding, lean forwards and do not pull back on the reins. If you do, the pony may fall over backwards. As the pony brings its feet back to the ground, ride forwards with determination.

PULLING
If a pony pulls, have its teeth checked and make sure that its bit fits correctly. Get expert advice to find out if you need to use a different bit or noseband. Practise riding between a walk and a trot in the riding arena, using your voice as well as other aids. While doing this, give and take on the reins – don't just pull on them.

DIFFICULT TO MOUNT
If a pony is difficult to mount, ask someone to stand at the pony's head and hold the bridle. Use a mounting block instead of mounting from the ground, so there is no chance of the saddle being pulled over. Be careful not to dig your toe into a pony's ribs as you get on.

HANDLING PROBLEMS

PULLS WHEN LED
If your pony pulls, practise leading it in an enclosed area and make sure it understands your voice commands. Use a bridle, or a controller headcollar, which applies pressure when a pony pulls and slackens when it stops pulling. When leading, pull and then slacken the reins or headcollar; do not pull constantly.

A pony should come when you show it food.

DIFFICULT TO CATCH

BARGES OUT OF THE STABLE
Make sure the stable doorway is not too narrow – if a pony has banged against it at some time, it may rush out through fear. Use a bridle or controller headcollar to give you more control. Reward a pony for good behaviour, and practise until it has gained confidence.

DIFFICULT TO LOAD
The horsebox must be light and inviting, with a safe, stable ramp. Allow plenty of time to practise when loading. Put protective boots on the pony and wear a hat, safe boots, and gloves yourself. Some ponies gain confidence from following an experienced one. Don't give up!

DIFFICULT TO CATCH
Leave a leather or safety headcollar on a pony that is difficult to catch. Reward it with food when it comes to you. Catch the pony regularly, reward it, and then release it immediately so it does not think that being caught always means work. Catch other ponies first, so that the pony has no friends left in the field.

KICKING
Never stand directly behind a pony whether it kicks or not. If a pony is prone to kicking, try to find out why it kicks. Problems are often caused when girths are tightened too roughly. If this is not the case and it still kicks, speak sharply to the pony. Keep ponies that kick other ponies at a safe distance when being ridden.

FIRST AID AND SAFETY

TO RIDE SAFELY you must make the right preparations, choose the correct clothes and equipment, and know what to do in an emergency. Always check that the pony's shoes and tack are in good condition, and never use damaged equipment. Learn the basics of first aid for both horses and people. This will help you to stay calm in an emergency when others may need your help.

Bag containing essentials can be fastened around the rider's waist.

FIRST-AID KIT
One rider in a group should carry a basic first-aid kit. This should include a hoofpick in case a pony gets a stone lodged in its hoof. If available, take a mobile phone – switched off – for emergencies.

Riding out safely
Before leaving the stable always tell someone where you are going and when you plan to be back. If you are riding a pony for the first time, go out with a friend whose pony is quiet and reliable. Ride out in daylight only, and do not gallop on verges or pedestrian rights of way.

Hat cover is made from fluorescent, reflective material.

Tack should be in good condition, particularly stitching on the reins, girths, and stirrup leathers.

Always ride on the correct side of the road, facing oncoming traffic.

BEING SEEN
Make sure that other road users can see you from as far away as possible, so that they have a chance to slow down and pass safely. Always wear fluorescent, reflective clothing, such as tabards and hat covers on dull or rainy days. It is sensible to wear fluorescent clothing in all weather conditions on busy roads.

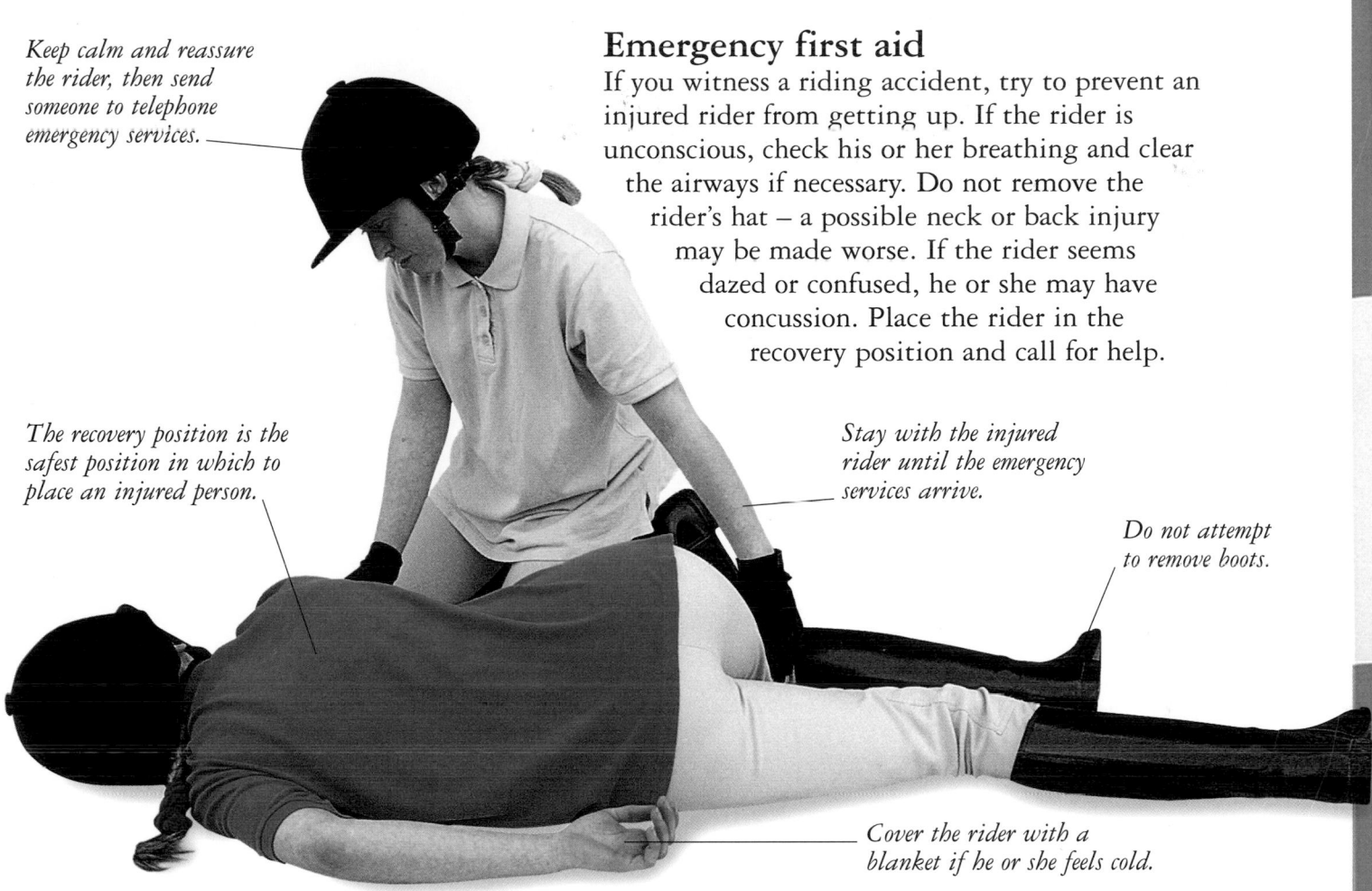

Keep calm and reassure the rider, then send someone to telephone emergency services.

Emergency first aid

If you witness a riding accident, try to prevent an injured rider from getting up. If the rider is unconscious, check his or her breathing and clear the airways if necessary. Do not remove the rider's hat – a possible neck or back injury may be made worse. If the rider seems dazed or confused, he or she may have concussion. Place the rider in the recovery position and call for help.

The recovery position is the safest position in which to place an injured person.

Stay with the injured rider until the emergency services arrive.

Do not attempt to remove boots.

Cover the rider with a blanket if he or she feels cold.

Attending to horse injury

You may need to attend to an injured horse when you are out for a ride. If a fracture is suspected, keep the horse still and call the vet immediately. If blood is spurting from a wound, a main artery has probably been severed. Apply a clean pressure pad to minimize bleeding and call the vet.

1 Dress the wound
Gently clip hair from the edges of the wound and wash away any dirt with clean water. Place a sterile, non-stick dressing with padding over the wound.

Place padding over the dressing before using a bandage.

2 Secure the padding
Keep the padding in place with a self-adhesive bandage. Keep pressure even, but do not pull the bandage too tight.

Start at the top to secure padding, then move down to wound area.

Hold the leg firmly with one hand.

3 Finish off
Bandage the leg so that you leave an edge of padding at the top and bottom. Change the dressings twice a day to prevent the wound from becoming infected.

HORSE
&PONY
CARE

CONFORMATION, COLOURS, AND MARKINGS

TO DESCRIBE OR ASSESS A HORSE, look at its conformation, coat colour, and any markings. Good conformation, or shape, means that the horse has correct proportions. Different breeds and types have different characteristics, but the guidelines for good conformation are always the same.

Points of a Horse

The points of the horse are names given to parts of its head, body, and limbs. They are like reference points on a map. Some parts have unusual names, such as the withers, so many people find it useful to learn all the points of a horse.

Crest

Poll

Ears

Forelock

Mane

Dock

Croup

Loins

Back

Shoulder

Withers

Throat

Chin groove

Mouth

Jugular groove

Windpipe

Shoulders that are powerful and sloping are found in more athletic horses. This feature makes them more comfortable to ride.

Breast

Stifle

Flank

Ribs

Belly

Thigh

Elbow

Forearm

Gaskin

Chestnut

Knee

Hock

Fetlock joint

Cannon bone

Heel

Pastern

Ergot

Coronet

Wall of hoof

Feet are shock absorbers so they must be well cared for.

CONFORMATION

A HORSE'S CONFORMATION
Good conformation means more than good looks. If a horse is well made, it will stand up to hard work because there is less strain on its body and limbs. Judging conformation takes practice, but in general a horse's body should look symmetrical. All horses have strong and weak points, but ideally the strong compensate for the weak.

Back must be strong to carry rider

Both pairs of legs should be straight with the feet pointing forward.

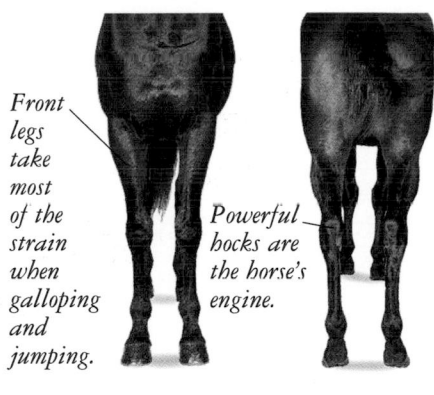

Front legs take most of the strain when galloping and jumping.

Powerful hocks are the horse's engine.

BASIC COLOURS

BASIC COAT COLOURS
Coat colours are either solid or broken. Colour is often used to describe a horse. It does not affect a horse's performance, but many people have preferences. Some breeds, such as the Cleveland Bay and Suffolk Punch, are always the same colour – Clevelands are bay and Suffolk Punches are chestnut. Appaloosas have spotted coats in varied patterns, such as blanket and snowflake. Grey horses vary from white to dark grey and can be plain, dappled, or flea-bitten.

CHESTNUT   GREY   BAY

DUN   PALOMINO   SKEWBALD

FACE MARKINGS

FACE MARKINGS
Natural patterns of white hair on a horse's face range from those covering the forehead and front of the face to small snips around the mouth. Some horses have more than one face marking, such as a star and snip.

STRIPE   STAR   BLAZE   SNIP

LEG MARKINGS

LEG MARKINGS
Leg markings are usually white. If they come to below the knee or hock they are called socks. If they extend further up the leg they are known as stockings. Black spots on white hair around the coronet are called ermine markings. Hooves can be black, white, or black with white stripes.

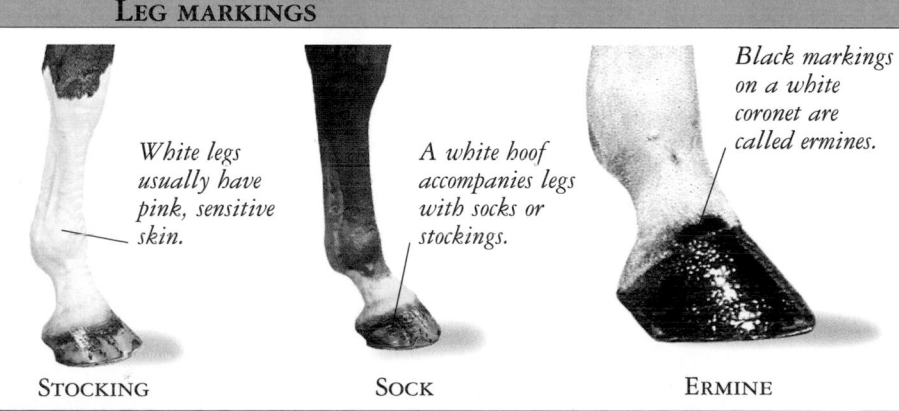

White legs usually have pink, sensitive skin.

A white hoof accompanies legs with socks or stockings.

Black markings on a white coronet are called ermines.

STOCKING   SOCK   ERMINE

CARING FOR A HORSE OR PONY

LOOKING AFTER A HORSE OR PONY is a big responsibility. A pony needs someone to provide food, shelter, and water, and to keep it fit and healthy. As you spend time mucking out the stable and grooming a pony, you will learn more about its habits and body language and will be able to assess how it is feeling. Taking care of a pony involves hard work throughout the year, but building a relationship with a pony can be very rewarding.

CHOOSE A PONY CAREFULLY
Try to spend time with different horses and ponies. This will help you to avoid making mistakes when deciding which type would suit you best.

Treat a pony gently as if it is a friend. Loud noises may frighten it.

Ears pointing forward show that the pony is interested and happy with its surroundings.

Look for a kind, friendly expression on the pony's face.

Choose a pony that is the right size for you. A pony that is too big may be difficult to handle.

Horses and ponies have a variety of colours and markings.

Check pony's feet daily.

A suitable pony
You need to build a partnership with the pony you look after. It should be the right temperament and size for you to handle easily. If this is your first experience with a pony, look for a kind, friendly one. Watch it carefully and learn to understand its signals. A pony that is nervous or difficult needs expert handling.

Many young riders start by helping out at a riding school.

Helping out

One of the best ways of learning how to look after a pony is to help at a local riding stables. You can learn how to muck out stables, groom, and handle different types of horses and ponies, with experienced people to help you. Spending time at a riding school will help you decide whether you enjoy the commitment before you own or share a pony.

Grooming kit

Every horse or pony should have its own grooming kit. Wash the brushes regularly and rinse them thoroughly to keep them clean. Do not use one pony's brushes on another, or you might spread skin infections. A grass-kept pony does not need much grooming as it needs to retain grease in its coat to protect it from the cold and rain. A stabled pony should be groomed more thoroughly.

Mucking out

Stables should be cleaned out every day. A four-pronged fork is useful for lifting dirty straw bedding. For mucking out a shavings bed use a shavings fork. This allows clean bits of shavings to fall through the gaps, while catching any wet material and droppings. Some tools for mucking out can also be used to remove droppings from fields. Remember to put your tools away when you have finished with them.

Hoof dressing

Body brush

Metal curry comb

Plastic curry comb

Mane comb

Pulling comb

Sweat scraper

Hoof pick

Sponges for the eyes, mouth, and nose, and another for the dock

Stable rubber

Rubber curry comb

Dandy brush

Yard broom

Shovel for picking up small bits of dirty bedding

Wheelbarrow for collecting muck

Waterproof boots

Shavings fork

Rake for raking gravel yard

Straw fork

Pitchfork, sometimes used for laying out straw bed.

Small rake and skep for picking up droppings

HANDLING A HORSE

HORSES AND PONIES respond best to quiet, confident handling. Keep movements smooth, and be gentle but positive when you touch a horse. Horses are worried by sudden movements and loud noises; use your voice in a soothing tone to calm and speak sharply, but not loudly, to reprimand.

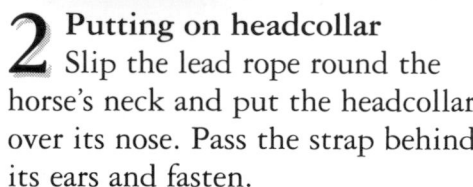

Be careful not to flip the headcollar over the horse's head and startle it.

The headcollar should be fastened securely but not too tightly.

Catching a horse

Take your time when trying to catch a horse. Even if you are in a hurry, try to give the impression that you have plenty of time. It is a good idea to occasionally catch a horse, reward it, then let it go, so it does not always associate being caught with being ridden.

2 Putting on headcollar
Slip the lead rope round the horse's neck and put the headcollar over its nose. Pass the strap behind its ears and fasten.

1 Approaching the horse
Approach the horse from one side at a slight angle, so that it can see you. Stay relaxed so that your body language invites the horse to come towards you.

Keep headcollar low and still as you approach.

Allow the horse to smell you. You may also want to reward the horse with a treat, so that it is willing to be caught.

Turning a horse out

Open the gate wide enough for easy access and shut it before you let the horse go. Before releasing the horse, turn its head towards the gate, so that you do not get kicked by its hind legs if it gallops off.

Body language

Watch horses in the field to study their body language. Ears pointing back warn others to stay away. Groups of horses determine their own positions of authority, from the leaders to followers.

Flattened ears show tension.

How to tie a quick-release knot

When tying up a horse, tie the lead rope to a string loop so that if the horse panics the string will break. A quick-release knot is also used to tie up haynets.

1 Start of knot
Loop rope through ring. Bring the loose end around and across so that you have made a slanting figure of eight.

This end of the rope attaches to the headcollar.

2 Making the knot
Pass the loose end behind both thicknesses of rope and then back through the bottom loop of your figure of eight.

Keep loops big so that the rope passes through easily.

3 Secure the knot
Push the loose end back through the loop to make another one. Pull down on the loop you have just made to tighten the knot.

This is a secure but safe quick-release knot.

4 To undo the knot
To undo the knot, pull on the loose end of the rope. This knot allows you to release a panicking horse quickly and safely.

Pull on loose end.

TYING UP A HORSE
When tying up a horse, allow enough length of rope for it to move its head. Some may pull back if they are tied up too short.

Tie lead rope to piece of string for safety.

OUT IN THE FIELD

ALL HORSES AND PONIES should be turned out every day to graze and relax. Some can live out permanently, while others need stabling part of the time. Ponies that have had laminitis should not be turned out on rich spring grass or they may get it again. Horses need fields with safe fencing and gates, clean water, shelter and other horses for company. A field must be large enough to supply all the horses within it enough grass on which to graze and space to roam.

FENCES AND GATES
Gates should be properly balanced and easy to open and close when leading horses through. There are many safe types of fencing, such as post and rail. Never use barbed wire or your horse may injure itself. Check fencing for breakages every day.

The ideal field

An individual horse needs at least 2 hectares (1 acre) of land on which to graze. Try to graze your horse on grass that has been grown especially for horses – cattle pasture may be too rich. Shelter to protect a horse from wind and rain, and to shade it in summer, can be provided by trees and hedges, or a field shelter. Get expert advice on field management, such as fertilising and resting land.

Post and rail fencing is safe and strong. Replace broken or weak rails immediately.

Try and use a field where someone nearby can keep an eye on the horses.

Grass should be weed free.

Poisonous plants

Check the field regularly for poisonous plants. Ragwort is particularly dangerous. It has yellow flowers and should be pulled up and burnt immediately – this will help to stop them growing again. Yew, acorns, and deadly nightshade are also dangerous when eaten. Call your vet if you suspect a horse has been poisoned.

Acorn attached to oak leaf   *Yew leaves*

FRESH WATER

There must always be plenty of clean, fresh water. Use a special water trough or a safe container with no sharp edges. Keep the trough clean and free from things that could contaminate the water, and from ice in winter.

Horses will go thirsty rather than drink dirty or contaminated water.

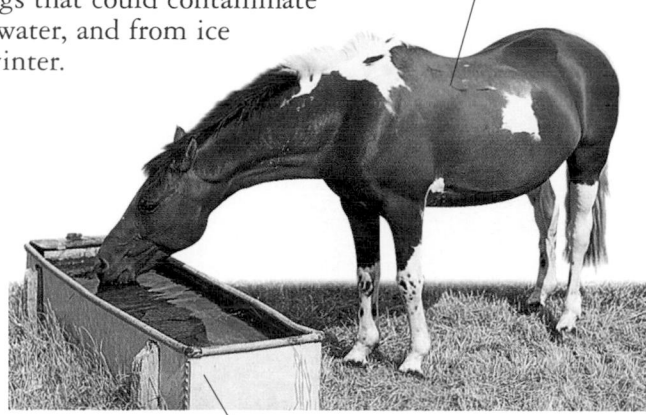

Water trough should not have sharp edges as these could injure horse.

Field shelters must have openings large enough to allow more than one horse to go through at a time. If your field slopes, put your shelter on the highest point so rain drains away from the site.

Fresh drinking water is supplied in a trough.

Trees and thick hedging provide all year round protection.

Lighting to help see on dark winter nights.

49

CARE OF A PONY AT GRASS

PONIES LIVING OUTDOORS in a field need daily care and attention, since they have special needs at different times of year. For example, they need protection from insects in summer and from cold weather in winter. Check a grass-kept pony for injury or illness, and make sure that shelter and clean water are always available and the fencing is safe.

Security measures
Freeze marking is a security system that can help trace a stolen pony. The mark is frozen onto the pony's skin but does not hurt. Each freeze mark is unique. Other systems of identification are hoof branding, identichipping, and lip tattooing.

Horse is identified by the number.

Checking the pony
Go and look over the pony at least once every day. A healthy pony is alert and not shivering. Make sure there are no signs of injury or illness and that its shoes and feet are in good condition. Look out for cuts and any signs of heat or swelling – small cuts may be hidden by a thick coat. Some ponies have pink skin around their noses that may get sunburnt in the summer, so use some protective cream.

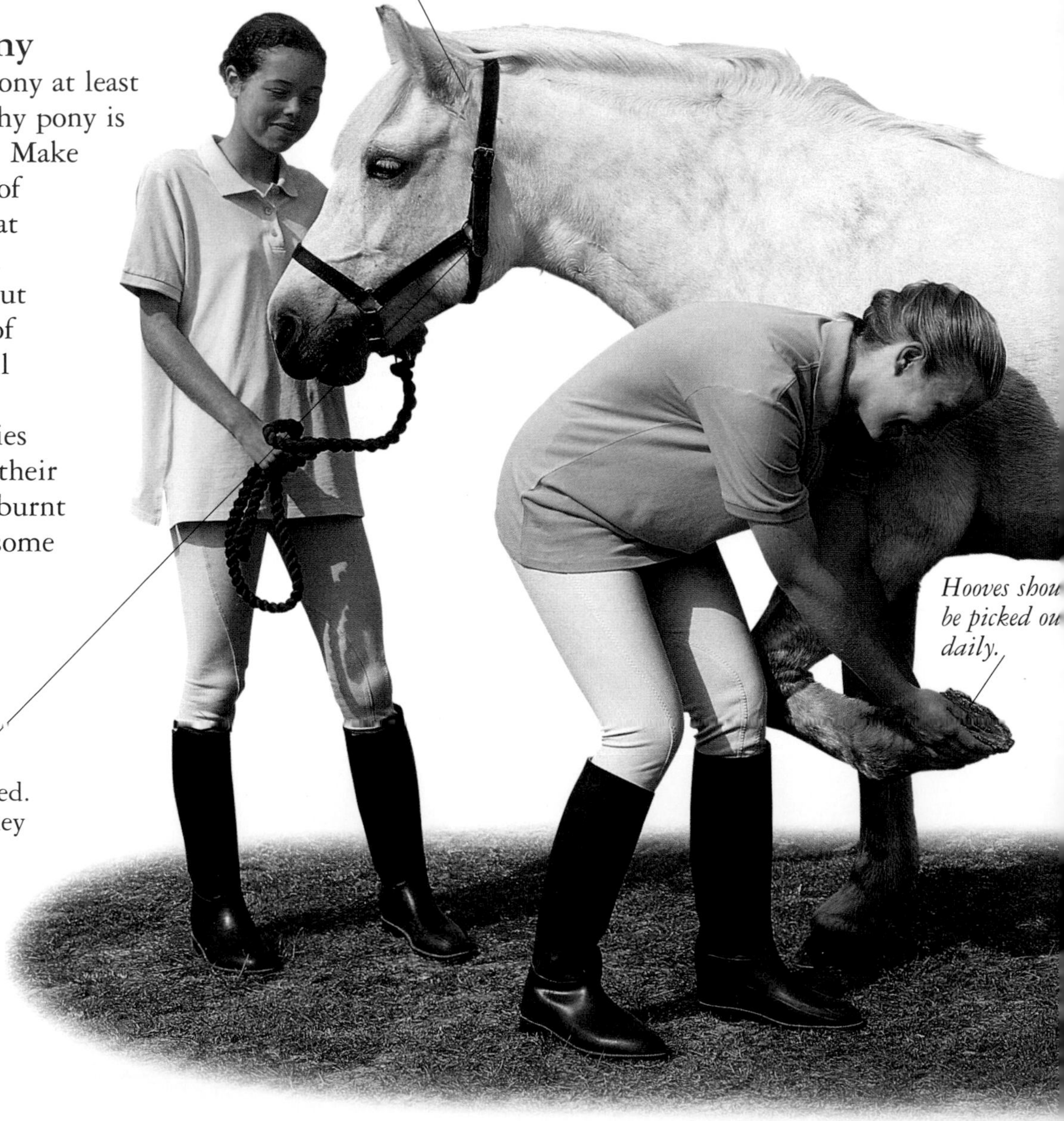

Base of ears should be warm.

Hooves shou[ld] be picked ou[t] daily.

Leather headcollars or ones with a breakable safety insert should be used. If these get caught up, they are pulled off without injuring the pony.

Seasonal needs

A pony that lives outdoors needs different kinds of protection at different times of year. It is important that shelter is available all year round, to give shade in the summer and protection from wind and rain in the winter.

A waterproof rug can help give protection in the winter.

SUMMER NEEDS
Insects are the biggest problem in the summer. Some bite and can cause allergic reactions. Insect repellent helps to control them. You can also use a fly fringe, fastened to a headcollar, which helps to keep insects away from the pony's eyes.

Fly fringe protects pony's eyes from flies.

WINTER NEEDS
Outdoor rugs protect the pony from cold, wind, and rain. Check rugs fit correctly and don't rub. Make sure you have two rugs in case one gets torn.

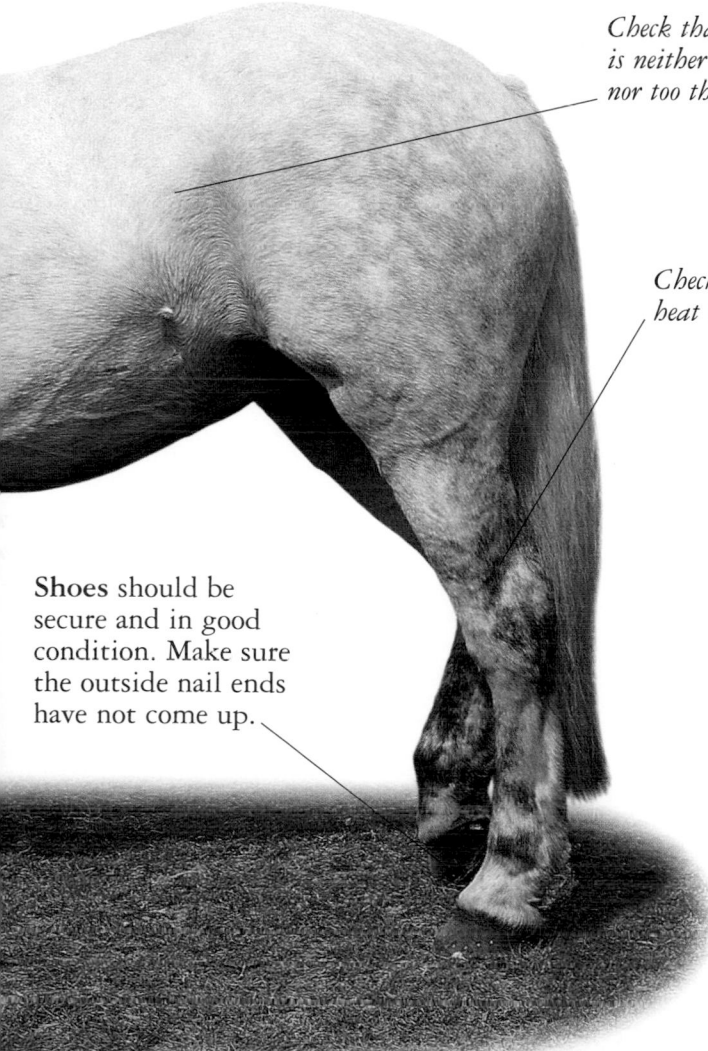

Check that the pony is neither too fat nor too thin.

Check legs for heat or swelling.

Shoes should be secure and in good condition. Make sure the outside nail ends have not come up.

Removing droppings regularly from the field is essential to protect a pony's health.

Fork through muck you can't pick up.

Fill in any holes in the field.

Field care

Remove droppings from the field as often as possible. This helps to reduce the amount of worm eggs on the field and to protect the pony's health. Also, pull up any poisonous plants, such as ragwort, and take them away to be destroyed.

THE STABLE YARD

THE IDEAL STABLE YARD is designed so that the horses are healthy, happy, and safe and so that the design is convenient for people using the yard. There may be outdoor stables or stables inside a large building called an American barn. Feed, hay, and bedding should be stored near the stables, but not so close as to become a fire risk. The yard must be fitted with safety and security precautions.

AMERICAN BARN
American barns allow you to muck out and groom out of bad weather. They must have wide central walkways for tying up and leading out horses, and good ventilation and drainage. There should be large doors at each end, which should be left open when possible. Fire precautions are vital inside barns.

Stable design
Stables must be light and large enough for a horse to walk round comfortably. Mares with foals need extra large stables. Good ventilation and drainage are important for a horse's health. Ideally there will be windows at the front and back and ventilation at roof height. Pitched roofs provide more air space, and are therefore preferable to flat roofs.

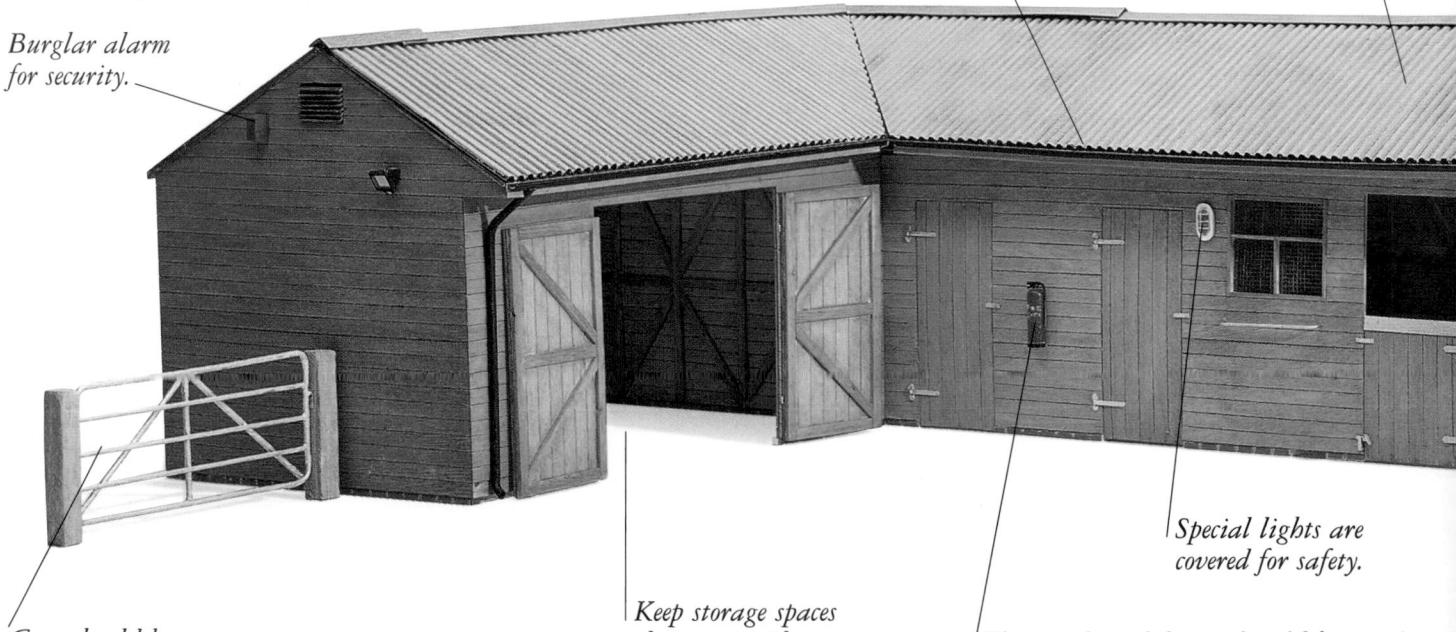

Pitched roof gives more room for air to circulate.

Gutter must be kept clear of falling leaves and other blockages.

Burglar alarm for security.

Special lights are covered for safety.

Gate should be shut to prevent horses escaping from yard.

Keep storage spaces clean to avoid attracting mice and rats.

Fire extinguishers should be easily seen and ready to use. Ask local fire officers for fire prevention advice.

Bedding materials

Wheat straw is a popular choice for bedding, but it contains a small amount of dust, which makes some horses cough. Paper, wood shavings, hemp, and rubber matting are alternative choices.

SHAVINGS   NEWSPAPER

RUBBER MATTING   STRAW

Roof ventilators help keep air clean and healthy.

Muck heap should be kept tidy.

Mucking out tools should be stored neatly.

Top half of stable door always left open to help ventilation.

Mucking out

Cleaning a stable is called mucking out and it must be done every day. Muck out completely if you use straw. Shavings, paper, and hemp are more absorbent, so remove droppings daily and do a full muck out once or twice a week. If you can, take the horse out of the stable before you begin.

1 Remove dirty straw
To muck out a straw bed, use a four-pronged fork to remove droppings and wet, dirty straw. Separate out the clean bedding, then shovel up and put the dirty bedding into a wheelbarrow.

Dirty bedding is heavy, so only lift a little at a time.

2 Brushing up
Sift through the remaining straw with your fork to check that it is clean. Pile it up round the sides and brush the floor thoroughly. Try to sprinkle some disinfectant on the bare floor once a week.

Add fresh bedding, piling it higher round the edges.

3 Laying down a bed
Fork piled up straw into the centre of the floor and check that the sides of the stable are clean. Pile fresh straw high around the sides of the stable wall to give added protection to the horse.

THE STABLED PONY

KEEPING A HORSE or pony in a stable allows you to control what it eats and enables you to keep it clean and healthy. However, looking after a stabled horse or pony takes a lot of time and work and requires you to follow a strict routine. All stabled horses and ponies should be turned out to grass for at least part of the day to keep them happy and relaxed.

Use your voice firmly but quietly. Some ponies will respond to your voice commands alone.

Stable manners

Ponies must be taught to behave well so they are safe to handle in the confined space of a stable. Teach them to step back or move away from you when you apply gentle pressure and use voice commands.

Anti-weave grid helps to stop pony from weaving over the door.

STABLE VICES
Ponies who do not like being confined may develop behavioural problems, or stable vices. These include swaying their heads from side to side, called weaving, or biting the stable door, called crib-biting. Ponies with stable vices may be happier when turned out to grass.

Hand pressure and voice commands tell the pony to step back. Apply the pressure as short nudges.

Boots, especially ones with protective toecaps, are safer than shoes or trainers.

SAFE CONTROL
Your pony should be happy to obey your commands in the stable. It is important to allow your pony some times of peace and quiet, such as during feed times.

DAILY ROUTINE

Ponies need a routine to remain healthy and happy. This means feeding them at the same time each day and giving them daily exercise. The combined system can be used where a pony is put out to grass during the day and kept in a stable at night.

TIME	STABLE KEPT PONY
7.00 AM	Check for any signs of illness or injury. Adjust rugs if necessary and give fresh water and first feed.
7.45 AM	Tie up pony outside stable and muck out. Pick out hooves, remove rugs, and brush over. Exercise now or at a time that suits you, allowing one hour after pony has been fed.
9.15 AM	Tack up and ride out or school. Walk for the last 15 minutes of exercise to allow pony to cool down. Brush over or wash if sweaty, then put on outdoor rug if weather is bad. Check hooves and shoes and turn out. Wash mangers and buckets.
12.00 PM	Bring in and give full groom. Put on stable rugs. Give second feed and hay and check water. *Put hay in hay net and hang in stable.*
2.00 PM	Check water, give more hay if necessary. Remove droppings from stable (skep out).
5.00 PM	Skep out and check water. Add or change rugs if necessary; remember temperature may drop at night. Give third feed and hay.
7.00 – 10.00 PM	Skep out and check water and rugs. Give fourth feed, if required, and more hay. *The stable must be clean for the night.*

TIME	COMBINED SYSTEM
7.00 AM	Check pony for illness or injury. Feed and leave to eat in peace. When finished, pick out hooves, put on outdoor rug if not riding, and turn out. Check water supply and fencing, and give hay in field if necessary. Muck out.
8.00 AM	Brush over and exercise. If pony has been turned out, allow half an hour after bringing in. Make sure pony is cool on return from exercise, brush over or wash down, and check hooves. Rug up if necessary and turn out. *Make sure the rug is fitted securely.*
4.00 PM	Bring in pony and check for signs of injury. Pick out hooves and check shoes. Brush over, change rugs if necessary, and give hay. If wet, use breathable rug that will transfer moisture away from body. Check one hour later and again if necessary. Change rugs so pony is dry and comfortable for the night.
5.00 PM	Check that pony is dry and warm enough. Give second feed and check water.
7.00 – 9.00 PM	Make sure pony is comfortable. Skep out and check water. Give hay and third feed if necessary.

FOOD AND FEEDING

HORSES NATURALLY EAT GRASS and hay, which is called forage. Forage must be of good quality since it is the main part of a horse's diet. When horses have a lot of exercise, they may need extra feed such as coarse mix or cubes. Small, frequent meals are better for a horse's digestive system than large ones, and allow one hour after feeding before you ride. Make sure clean water is always available.

Feed your horse small amounts often.

The right amount
A horse needs between 1.5 and 2.5 per cent of its bodyweight in food for a day. For example a 300 kg (660 lbs) pony would need about 7.5 kg (16.5 lbs) food every day. Forage (grass and hay) should provide at least half, and usually more, of the total amount. If a horse is being worked hard, you may need to increase its feed in line with its work. Ask an expert if you are unsure of how much to feed.

Horses can be fed from a bucket or manger.

Feeding hay
Hay can be fed on the ground, in a haynet, or in a rack. Soaking hay in clean water helps prevent coughing. If soaking hay, submerge for up to one hour. Never feed a horse dusty or mouldy hay.

1 Filling haynet
To fill a haynet, hold the top open with one hand and put hay in with the other. Be careful the string around the hay bale doesn't get tangled with the hay.

Shake hay to remove dust.

Pull net to correct height.

2 Placing haynet
Pass haynet drawstring through tying-up ring and pull the net up. This prevents the horse from getting its foot caught in an empty haynet.

WHAT TO FEED

Feed pellets or coarse mix (compound feeds), or cereals, such as oats. Compound feeds are best since they are specially formulated; don't add cereals, since they will alter the compound formula.

DIFFERENT FEEDS

MAIN FOODS
Oats and barley are traditional horse feeds. Flaked maize is fed only in small amounts to horses that are working hard. Bran should not be fed routinely – only feed it as a bran mash on your vet's advice. Sugar beet cubes are a good energy source but must be soaked in water for at least 12 hours before feeding.

BARLEY

FLAKED MAIZE

COARSE MIX

CUBES

BRAN

OATS

SOAKED SUGAR BEET

SUPPLEMENTS

EXTRAS
All horses should have salt licks available. Horses also enjoy fruit and vegetables, especially carrots and apples, sliced and added to their feed. Some horses may need vitamin and mineral supplements or extras such as cod liver oil. Always get expert advice before feeding these, since compound feeds already contain the vitamins and minerals a horse needs.

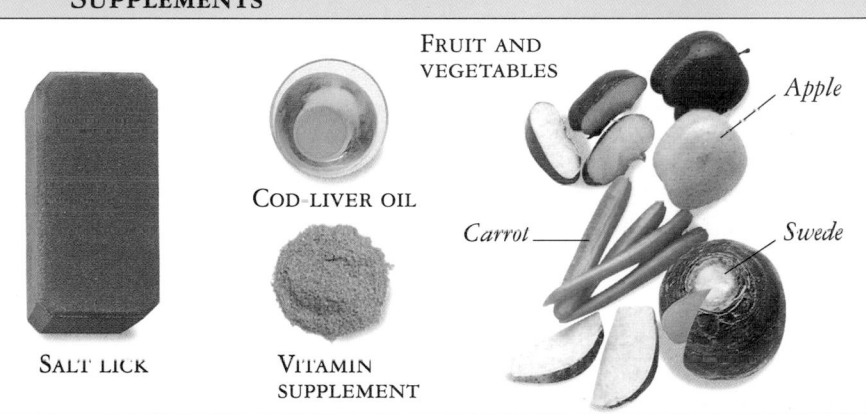

FRUIT AND VEGETABLES

Apple

COD-LIVER OIL

Carrot

Swede

SALT LICK

VITAMIN SUPPLEMENT

3 Tying up haynet
Take the end of the drawstring down to the bottom of the haynet and pass it through one of the holes, about two thirds of the way down the haynet. Pull the net up again.

Pull up net to tying-up ring.

Pass loose end through the knot so it can't be pulled undone.

4 Fasten knot
Pass the loose end of the drawstring behind the other piece and pull it through in a loop. Pull down with both hands to make a slip knot that is secure but easy to undo.

How to weigh a horse
To calculate a horse's approximate weight use a weigh tape, which measures a horse's girth. This gives corresponding weights to measurements and enables you to decide how much to feed your horse.

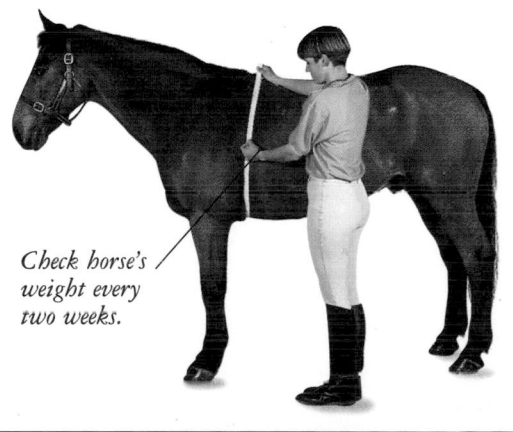

Check horse's weight every two weeks.

GROOMING

DAILY GROOMING helps keep a pony clean and its coat, skin, and feet healthy. Grooming also helps you get to know a pony and to feel for any problems, such as heat in the legs, that may occur. A grooming kit contains special tools, which are used for different purposes; keep it clean and only use it on the horse it belongs to.

Use hoof pick from heel to toe.

PICKING OUT FEET
Use a hoof pick to clean a pony's feet daily. Work downwards, from heel to toe, and do not dig into the V-shaped frog.

Use the hand nearest the horse's body to groom, since it is easier to to put your weight into the brush strokes.

Tie the pony up outside, so that dust from grooming doesn't affect its breathing.

How to groom
Begin grooming by loosening the dirt in the coat with a rubber curry comb or groomer. Use a dandy brush to flick off loose mud. Using short strokes, remove grease with a body brush. Brush the mane and tail with a body brush or an ordinary hairbrush to avoid breaking the hair. Finally clean the eyes, nose, and dock.

1 Brushing pony over
Before riding out, brush your pony over and pick out its feet. Make sure that there is no dirt or dried mud on parts of the pony where tack or rugs will rest, since this might rub. Check for mud on the back and girth areas, behind the elbows, the face, and the base of the ears.

USING A CURRY COMB
To clean the body brush scrape it against a metal curry comb, then knock out the dust from the curry comb. Never use metal curry combs on a pony.

2 Cleaning eyes, nose, and dock
Use separate sponges, or pieces of cotton wool, to clean the eyes, nose, and dock. Dampen the sponges or cotton wool, then gently wipe the necessary parts of the pony. If your pony has a runny nose or weeping eye there may be a problem, so ask an expert for advice.

Always wash the sponge after use.

58

Care of a grass-kept pony

Ponies that live outside need the natural grease in their coats to protect them from cold and wet. Before you ride a grass-kept pony, remove dried mud with a rubber curry comb, then brush over with a dandy or whisk brush. Do not use a body brush on the pony's coat since it takes out the grease; only use a body brush to tidy the mane and tail. Finally pick out the feet, and clean eyes, nose, and dock.

Thick coat has natural grease, which protects against wind and rain.

Bathing a pony

Only bath a pony on a warm day. Wet the coat, then work the shampoo into the pony's coat with a sponge or shampoo glove. Rinse thoroughly, then repeat if necessary. Once finished, walk pony around until it is dry.

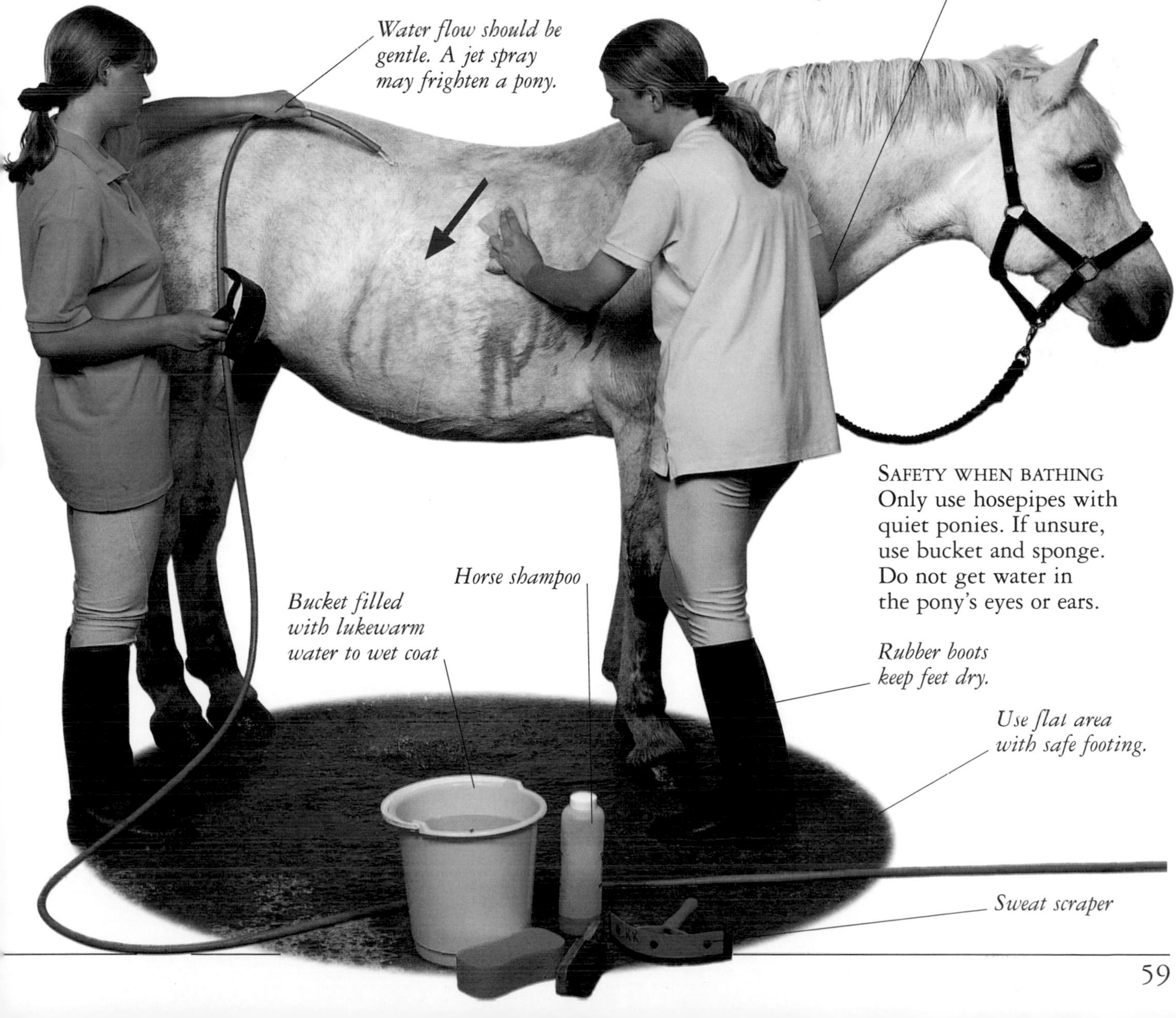

Helper should hold onto pony's lead rope if unsure of its reactions.

Water flow should be gentle. A jet spray may frighten a pony.

SAFETY WHEN BATHING
Only use hosepipes with quiet ponies. If unsure, use bucket and sponge. Do not get water in the pony's eyes or ears.

Rubber boots keep feet dry.

Horse shampoo

Bucket filled with lukewarm water to wet coat

Use flat area with safe footing.

Sweat scraper

59

MANES AND TAILS

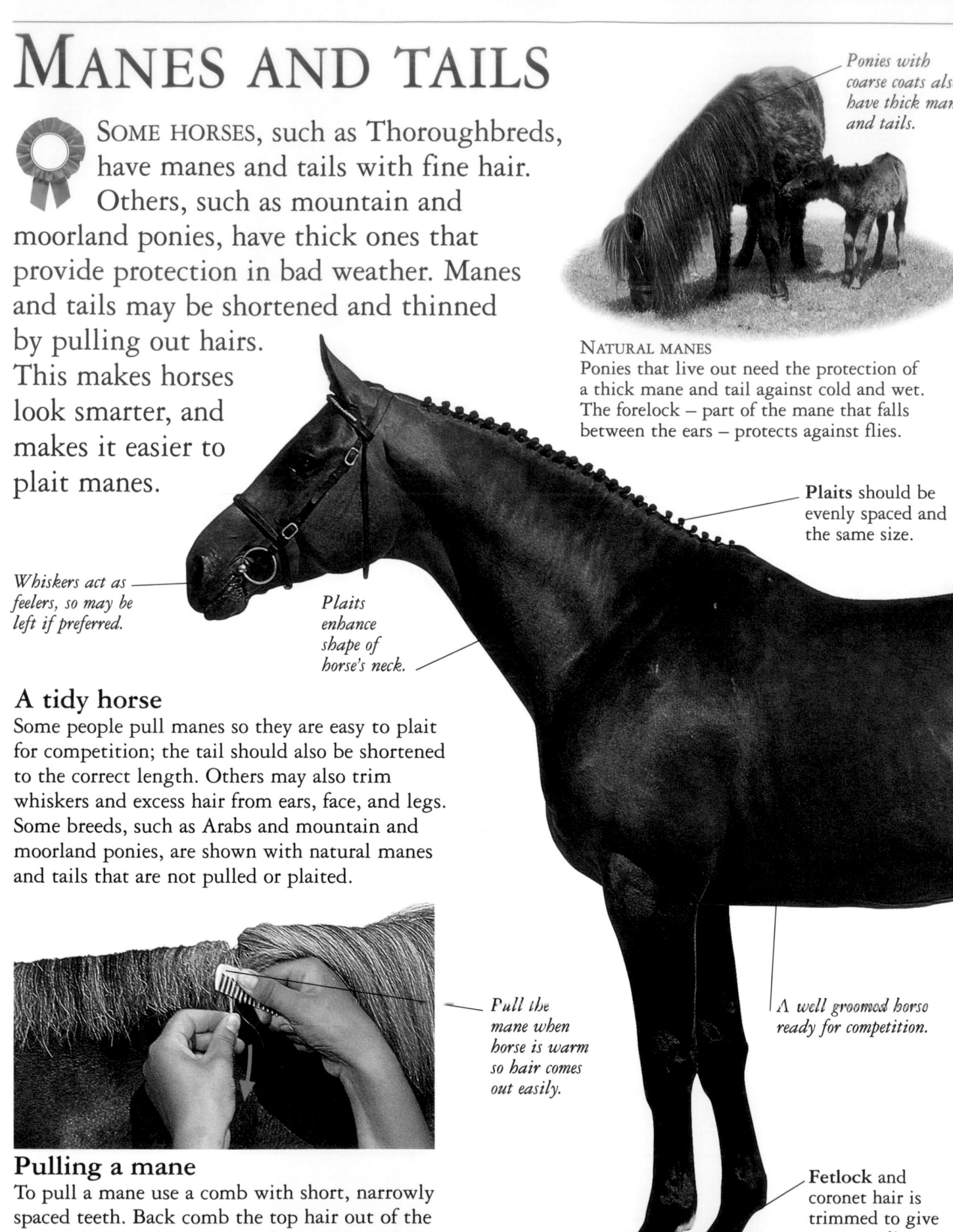

SOME HORSES, such as Thoroughbreds, have manes and tails with fine hair. Others, such as mountain and moorland ponies, have thick ones that provide protection in bad weather. Manes and tails may be shortened and thinned by pulling out hairs. This makes horses look smarter, and makes it easier to plait manes.

Ponies with coarse coats also have thick manes and tails.

NATURAL MANES
Ponies that live out need the protection of a thick mane and tail against cold and wet. The forelock – part of the mane that falls between the ears – protects against flies.

Plaits should be evenly spaced and the same size.

Whiskers act as feelers, so may be left if preferred.

Plaits enhance shape of horse's neck.

A tidy horse
Some people pull manes so they are easy to plait for competition; the tail should also be shortened to the correct length. Others may also trim whiskers and excess hair from ears, face, and legs. Some breeds, such as Arabs and mountain and moorland ponies, are shown with natural manes and tails that are not pulled or plaited.

Pull the mane when horse is warm so hair comes out easily.

A well groomed horse ready for competition.

Pulling a mane
To pull a mane use a comb with short, narrowly spaced teeth. Back comb the top hair out of the way and take hold of four or five underneath hairs. Pull these out with a sharp, downwards tug.

Fetlock and coronet hair is trimmed to give a neat outline.

Pulling a tail
Tail pulling creates a neat shape but some horses object to it. Stand to the side and pull three or four underneath hairs at a time from each side until you reach halfway down the dock (tail bones). If the horse is unhappy, stop in case you get kicked.

Trimming a tail
To trim a tail needs two people; one to hold out the tail at the angle it is carried when the horse moves, the other to cut. Cut straight across the bottom at the correct length. The top of a full tail – one that has not been pulled – can be plaited.

Pull quickly downwards.

Avoid pulling front of tail as hair will stick up as it grows.

Usual length is 10 cms (4 in) below the point of the hock.

Tail end should be level when horse is on the move.

Putting on a tail bandage
A tail bandage encourages the hair of a pulled tail to lie flat. It also protects the tail hair from being rubbed when travelling in a horsebox or trailer.

Start with bandage rolled so tapes are to the inside.

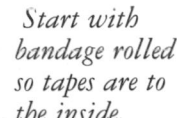

1 From the top
Start at the top and bandage down to the end of the tail bone. Keep pressure firm and even, but not too tight.

2 Tying up
Wrap tapes round, tie in a bow at the front and tuck in ends. Bend the tail gently into its normal position.

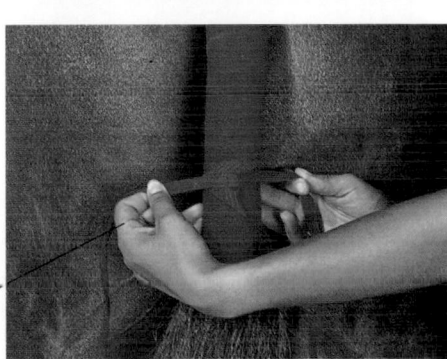

Tapes should be fastened no tighter than the bandage.

HOOVES AND SHOEING

A HORSE'S HOOVES, or feet, bear a lot of weight and help cushion the impact when a horse runs or jumps. In the wild, horses' hooves wear down naturally as they roam large distances, however domesticated horses need their hooves trimmed regularly by a farrier. Most working horses need metal shoes to protect their hooves on hard surfaces.

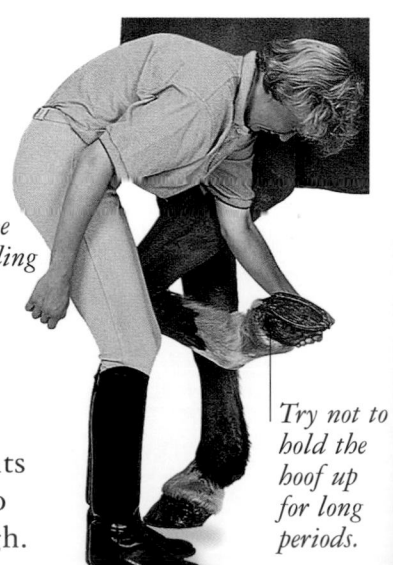

Rubbery frog absorbs jolts when hoof hits the ground.

Bar

Sole

Toe

Hard wall

UNDERSIDE OF THE HOOF
The sole should be slightly concave rather than flat to help the horse grip the ground. The V-shaped frog acts as a pump for the hoof's blood supply.

Parts of the hoof
The hoof is a hard outer shell that encases sensitive structures such as bones, blood vessels, and cartilage. The bottom part is made up of the sole and a V-shaped wedge called the frog.

The front hooves should be almost round.

Regular trimming keeps the hoof in shape and prevents splits.

FOOT CONFORMATION
Good foot conformation is when the front and hind hooves each form a pair that are the same size and shape.

How to check a horse's hooves
Check your horse's shoes and pick out its hooves once a day. Unpleasant smells, other than normal stable smells, are a sign of infection.

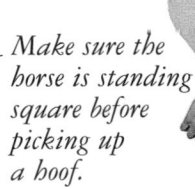

Keep your hand on the inside, not the outside of the horse's leg.

1 Check the leg
Stand to one side, and run your hand down the leg checking for abnormalities.

2 Get horse to pick up hoof
Squeeze the fetlock and use your voice to encourage the horse to pick up its hoof.

Make sure the horse is standing square before picking up a hoof.

3 Hold the hoof
As the horse lifts its hoof, catch the toe. Do not lift the leg too high.

Try not to hold the hoof up for long periods.

Dressing the hoof

Cosmetic hoof dressings give a shiny appearance to the hoof. They are used after grooming, for special occasions such as shows. Do not use hoof dressings without asking your farrier's or vet's advice, as some may not be suitable for your horse's feet.

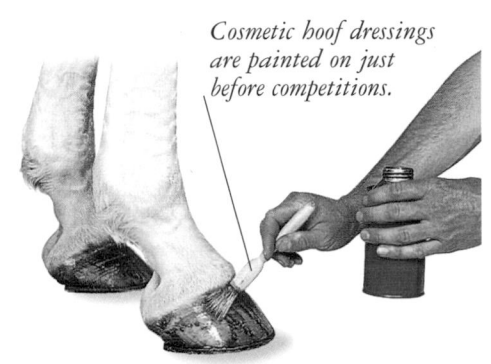

Cosmetic hoof dressings are painted on just before competitions.

Shoeing a horse

Horses are shod to enable them to work in comfort. Sometimes special studs are screwed into the shoes to give extra grip for jumping and galloping.

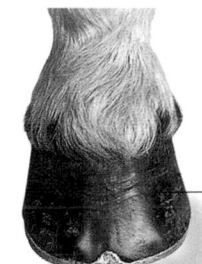

Horseshoe nails have flat, square heads.

Well-shaped hoof in good condition that has been recently shod

WHEN TO SHOE
Horses and ponies should have their shoes removed and their hooves trimmed every six weeks. Worn shoes should be replaced.

WELL-SHOD HOOF
The shoe should be shaped to fit the hoof, not the other way around. Nailing the shoes on does not hurt the horse.

The farrier

A farrier, who makes horseshoes and shoes horses, needs a dry, well-lit area in which to work. Horses can be shod cold or hot. Both methods use nails to keep the shoe in place, however during hot shoeing the shoe is burnt on, which often gives a better fit.

The farrier will appreciate a quiet, well-mannered horse.

Curved knife, called drawing knife, for trimming hoof.

Protective leather apron on which farrier can rest horse's leg.

Frog is sensitive and must not be punctured.

The horse should be ready when the farrier arrives, and have clean legs and hooves.

Hind hooves are slightly smaller than front hooves.

CLIPPING

HORSES ARE CLIPPED if their winter coats are too thick for them to work or be ridden without sweating. A horse may need several clips during one season. The type of clip depends on the horse's lifestyle and workload; the more work it does, the less winter coat it should have. A clipped horse needs to wear rugs indoors and out so that it is warm when not working. Some horses are nervous of being clipped, and must be handled by experts.

NATURAL COATS
All horses and ponies grow winter coats. Breeds such as British native ponies have thicker winter coats, as protection against wind and rain, than horses with a lot of Thoroughbred or Arab blood, which are kept in stables.

Types of clip
There are several different types of clip. Sometimes a lot of hair is removed from horses that work hard. Those that perform lighter work, or that spend most of their time outdoors, need some of their natural coat left on.

HUNTER CLIP
The hunter clip is used on horses that work hard and fast. All of the coat is clipped except that on the legs and sometimes under the saddle.

Thick leg hair protects the horse against mud and thorns.

BLANKET CLIP
Leaving a blanket-shaped area over the back of the horse unclipped helps keep the horse's back warm. Hair is also left on the legs, but is clipped off the neck. This type of clip allows a hard-working horse to keep cool.

Clipping a horse

Always clip a horse in a dry, light area, and never outdoors when it is wet or windy. Be careful when using electric clippers – they can be dangerous. Only experts should clip inexperienced or nervous horses.

Trim the hair from the edges of the horse's ears only, not inside.

Keep the folded rug on the pony so it does not get cold.

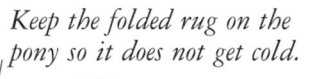

Clip in smooth sweeps against the direction of the hair growth.

Someone holds the horse and gives it confidence while another person clips.

Care of a clipped horse

A clipped horse must be kept warm and dry with rugs. If kept indoors, a horse must have a well-ventilated, but not draughty, space. Rugs with neck covers and tailflaps give extra protection. A fully-clipped horse may need to wear an exercise sheet when out riding.

Before putting the rug on remove loose hair.

Head is either clipped fully or clipped up to the bridle cheekpieces, with hair left on the front of the face.

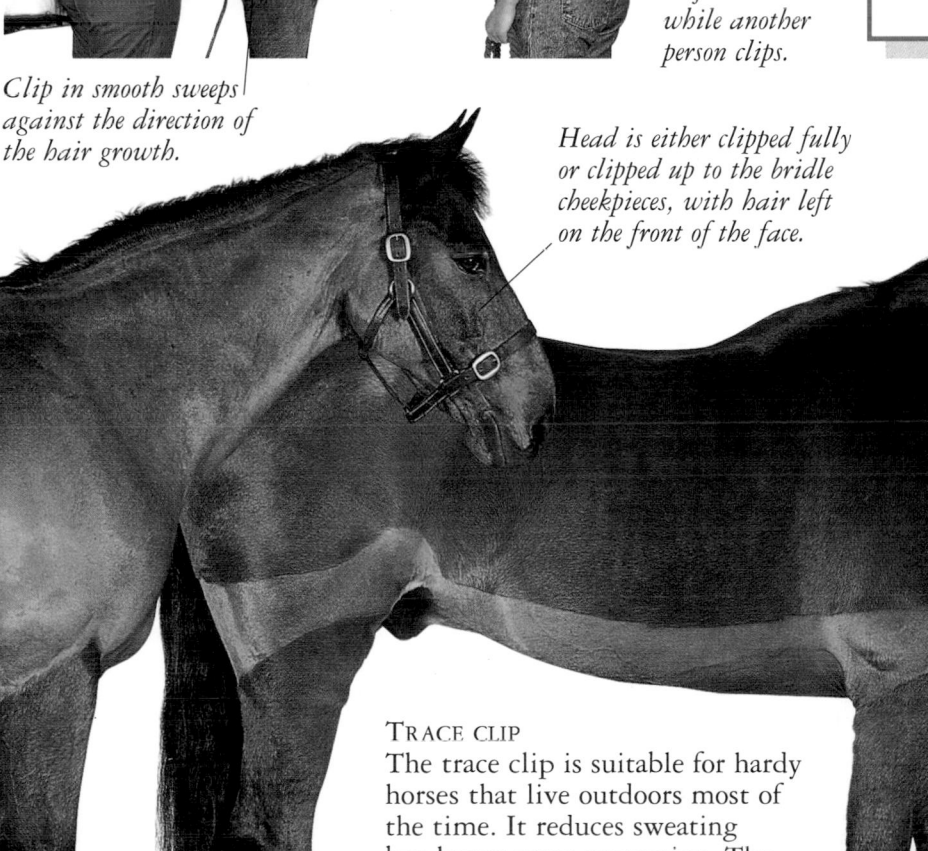

Coat is clipped off the underside of the neck, where horses often sweat.

TRACE CLIP
The trace clip is suitable for hardy horses that live outdoors most of the time. It reduces sweating but leaves some protection. The trace clip gets its name because it was designed for harness horses and follows the lines of the harness traces.

A trace-clipped horse may need to wear a rug when resting.

RUGS AND RUGGING UP

A RUG KEEPS A HORSE warm and dry in cold weather. In summer, light rugs can be used to protect horses from insects. Rugs also help to dry off a sweating horse, or if a horse is very wet, they can help it warm up and dry off more quickly. The main types of rug are outdoor or New Zealand rugs, stable rugs, summer sheets, coolers, and sweat sheets.

Putting on a rug

A horse's coat must lie flat under its rug so it is comfortable. The rug fastenings must be tight enough to keep the rug in place, but not so tight they restrict or cut into the horse.

Measuring up

A rug must be the correct size to stay in place. Measure the horse from the centre of its chest in a straight line across its body. This will give you the length your horse needs.

Give the measurements to a saddler, who will work out the size you need.

Modern rugs are machine washable. Keep them clean to prevent skin problems.

A high-cut rug on the neck will be less likely to slip backwards than one which is cut low on the neck.

1 Place the rug
Fold the rug in half from the back to the front and place it over the withers. Slide the rug back so the horse's coat lies flat underneath, and fold down the back half.

The rug should not press on the horse's chest.

Types of rug

There are many different types of rugs. A stable rug keeps the horse warm and clean. It is easy to wash and can be worn daily. Summer sheets are made of light cotton to keep dust and flies off a stabled, groomed horse. Sweat rugs and coolers allow the horse's sweat to evaporate.

Stable rugs do not need to be waterproof. You may need to use more than one rug on your horse as the weather gets very cold.

RUGS

• A well-fitting rug should not slip backwards or rub your horse

• Each horse should have its own rugs to avoid spreading infections

• Keep spare rugs in case one gets damaged

• Clean winter rugs before storing them

Outdoor or New Zealand rugs must be waterproof. They are available in canvas and many modern lightweight materials.

Summer sheets are usually made from cotton.

Traditional sweat sheets are used with a rug or summer sheet laid over the top, to trap a layer of air.

Rug should cover the withers at the front.

Cross surcingles help prevent excess pressure on horse's spine.

Some surcingles are elasticated.

2 Fasten the front straps
Fasten the rug leaving a hand's width between the rug and the horse's body.

3 Fasten the cross surcingles
The cross surcingles fasten around the horse's girth. Adjust the straps leaving a hand's width between them and the horse.

HEALTH AND FIRST AID

REGULAR WORMING, teeth rasping, and vaccinations against influenza and tetanus are vital to keep a horse healthy. Your vet can advise you about these. Learn to recognize when a horse might be ill, and how to take its temperature and check its pulse and respiration (breathing) rate. If in doubt or worried, always call a vet.

GAMGEE PADDING

SCISSORS

COLD TREATMENT PACK

ANTISEPTIC LIQUID

FIRST AID KIT
Keep a first aid kit at the stable and take it with you when you go to shows. Your vet will advise you what to include in the kit.

Eyes should be fully open and bright, with no discharge.

Checking your horse
Check your horse every day for signs of injury or illness. As you get to know your horse you will be able to tell if it is not well. A healthy horse is alert and appears happy.

A sore back can be a sign of a badly fitting saddle.

Tail should be relaxed, not clamped down.

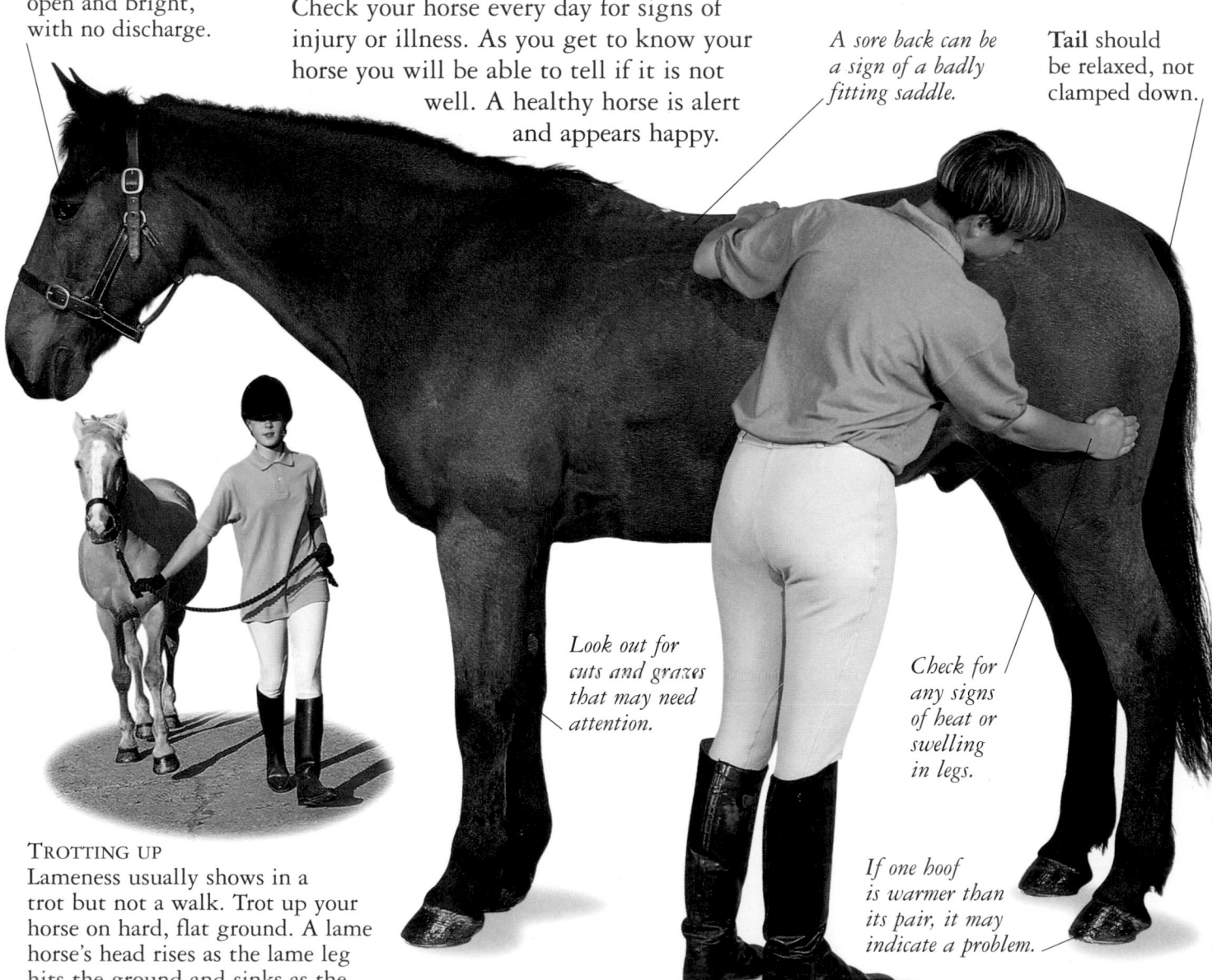

Look out for cuts and grazes that may need attention.

Check for any signs of heat or swelling in legs.

If one hoof is warmer than its pair, it may indicate a problem.

TROTTING UP
Lameness usually shows in a trot but not a walk. Trot up your horse on hard, flat ground. A lame horse's head rises as the lame leg hits the ground and sinks as the sound one comes down.

Preventing illness

It is better to prevent disease than to have to treat it once it occurs. All horses should be wormed and vaccinated regularly. They should also have their teeth checked and rasped at least once a year. Daily checks and correct management and feeding help to prevent illness.

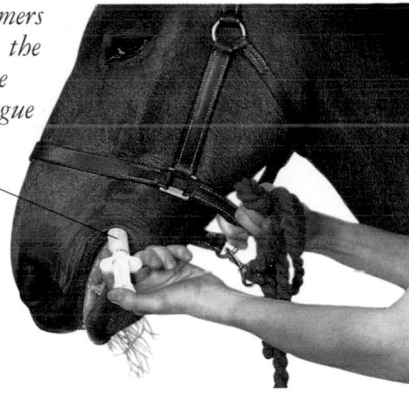

Paste wormers are put on the back of the horse's tongue using a syringe.

CHECKING PULSE
A normal pulse in an adult horse ranges between 35 and 45 beats per minute. The pulse will be faster in hot weather or when the horse has worked hard.

One of the easiest places to take the pulse is where the facial artery crosses the horse's jaw bone.

WORMING
Horses should be wormed every few weeks. There are many different types of worm; ask your vet's advice on which type of wormer to use and when to give them.

WHEN TO CALL THE VET

Always call the vet if you are worried about something, however small. Suspected colic or laminitis, or wounds spurting blood are always emergencies. A vet should always be called if lameness is severe or prolonged, or if a wound may need stitching.

COMMON AILMENTS

COLIC
Colic is another word for abdominal pain or stomach ache. Horses cannot be sick, so colic is always serious. Call your vet as soon as you suspect that something is wrong. Some cases may need surgery.

SIGNS OF COLIC

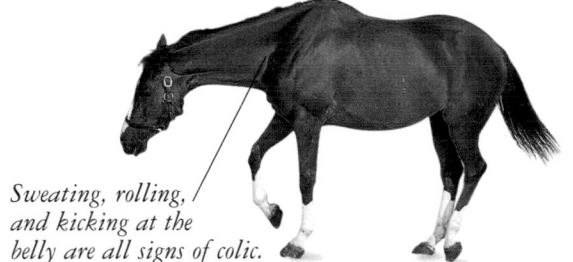

Sweating, rolling, and kicking at the belly are all signs of colic.

GENERALLY UNWELL
Always call your vet if you think your horse might need treatment. Describe the symptoms or injury carefully. With suspected illness, it may be useful to take the horse's temperature.

BAD CUT
Any cut that is longer than 2.5 cm (1 in) or gapes open may need stitching. Puncture wounds and those near joints may also need veterinary attention. Be safe, not sorry!

LAMINITIS
Laminitis is a painful hoof condition that is especially common in ponies. It is often linked to eating rich grass and usually affects the front hooves, so the pony tries to put more weight on its back ones. Your vet may recommend special shoes for your pony to wear.

ARTERIAL BLEEDING
If bright red blood spurts from a wound, your horse has probably severed an artery. Press a clean cloth firmly over the wound to limit the bleeding until the vet arrives.

PROLONGED LAMENESS
Always rest a lame horse. If very mild lameness lasts for more than two days, or if you are unsure, call your vet. Conditions such as tendon injuries or pulled muscles can get worse and need immediate treatment, so again, call your vet.

SITES OF LAMENESS

Most causes of lameness occur in the hoof, such as bruises and puncture wounds.

SEVERE LAMENESS
A horse that is badly lame or unable to put its injured hoof to the ground is an emergency case. With suspected fractures, try to keep the horse still until the vet arrives. This prevents the injury from getting worse.

CARE OF TACK

TACK MUST BE KEPT CLEAN and in good repair. Wash the bit and clean off dried mud every time you ride. If you don't take care of your tack it will become hard and cracked and uncomfortable for the horse to wear. At least once a week, more often if possible, dismantle the tack and clean thoroughly.

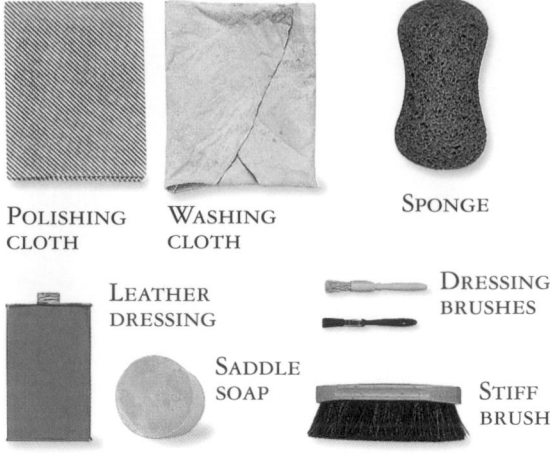

POLISHING CLOTH

WASHING CLOTH

SPONGE

LEATHER DRESSING

DRESSING BRUSHES

SADDLE SOAP

STIFF BRUSH

TACK CLEANING KIT
For general tack cleaning you need warm water, cloths and sponges, and a stiff brush to remove dirt. Use saddle soap to keep the tack supple, and apply leather dressing about once a month, especially if the tack is new.

Tack
Every horse should have its own tack. Make sure the tack fits properly; get expert advice if you are not sure. Saddles and bridles are made from either leather or synthetic materials. Keep tack in a dry, warm place, away from damp. Dry rain soaked leather tack away from direct heat otherwise it may turn brittle.

To hang a bridle use a special bridle rack or make your own from a round tin.

Wash bits in clean water.

Don't use metal polish on mouthpiece.

Only use saddle soap on leather reins.

Too much soap on the saddle seat may stain clothes.

Wash synthetic girths as often as is necessary.

Synthetic tack
Some synthetic tack, especially bridles and girths, comes in bright, cheerful colours. Synthetic tack should be wiped with a damp cloth or washed according to the manufacturer's instructions.

Do not use saddle soap or oil on synthetic tack.

Brush mud off synthetic tack.

Scrub dirt from stirrup treads, then wash and dry stirrup irons.

Remove girth for cleaning.

SADDLE CARE
Keep your saddle on a special rack or stand to help prevent it from getting damaged. As with all tack, the saddle should always be kept in a dry room.

In the tack room

Your tack room should be dry, warm, and secure. It is a good idea to install security equipment, such as alarms and a good lock. It is in the tack room that you usually clean the tack. To do this remove grease and dirt with a damp cloth, then apply saddle soap with a slightly damp sponge. Wash and rinse bits and stirrup irons, then polish with a dry cloth. Brush or wash girths and numnahs.

The pommel and cantle, at the front and back of a saddle, are easily damaged.

TACK CARE

- Check tack for wear every time you ride, especially areas where metal rests on leather

- Dirty tack can give pony skin infections, so clean tack often

- Apply saddle soap to both sides of the leather, but leather dressing to the underside, or flesh side, only

Bridles are easier to clean if hung from special bridle hooks.

Only put one saddle on each rack. Do not stack saddles.

Water should be warm, not hot.

When appling leather dressing, use a small brush.

Keep your saddle soap sponge damp but not wet. The soap should not foam up when you apply it.

TRANSPORTING A HORSE

WHEN TRANSPORTING a horse in a horsebox you must aways protect it with travelling equipment, even for short journeys. The horsebox or trailer should be in good condition and be large enough for a horse to travel comfortably. Horses should be tied up, but foals travel loose with their mothers. The driver should try to drive as smoothly as possible.

Protecting the horse
A horse should always wear travel boots or leg bandages put on over padding. A tail bandage or tailguard and a rug suitable for the weather conditions are also essential.

Rug protects horse from draughts in hot weather.

Loading up
When loading the horse into the horsebox, open up the vehicle as much as possible so the horse can see where it is being asked to go. Make sure the ramp is secure, then lead the horse straight up it. Look ahead into the box, not back at the horse. Tie the horse up so it cannot turn around.

The vehicle interior
should be light and inviting as horses do not like walking into dark places.

Provide a small haynet to prevent horse becoming bored during the journey.

WARNING!
Only load into an unhitched trailer if the rear prop stands are lowered.

Ramp must be stable, not tipped up at one side.

Check that tyre pressures are correct before every journey.

HORSE TRAVEL

- Always put travelling equipment on a horse, even for a short journey

- Vehicle should be light, airy, and in good condition

- Allow plenty of time for loading, unloading, and travelling so the horse is calm when it arrives

- Give the horse a haynet in the vehicle to encourage it to relax on the journey

- Driver should make all changes in speed and direction as smooth as possible

Unloading

The vehicle should be parked so that the horse has plenty of room to turn when it walks off the ramp. Make sure the ramp is stable, and lead the horse straight out so it does not bang against the side of the horsebox.

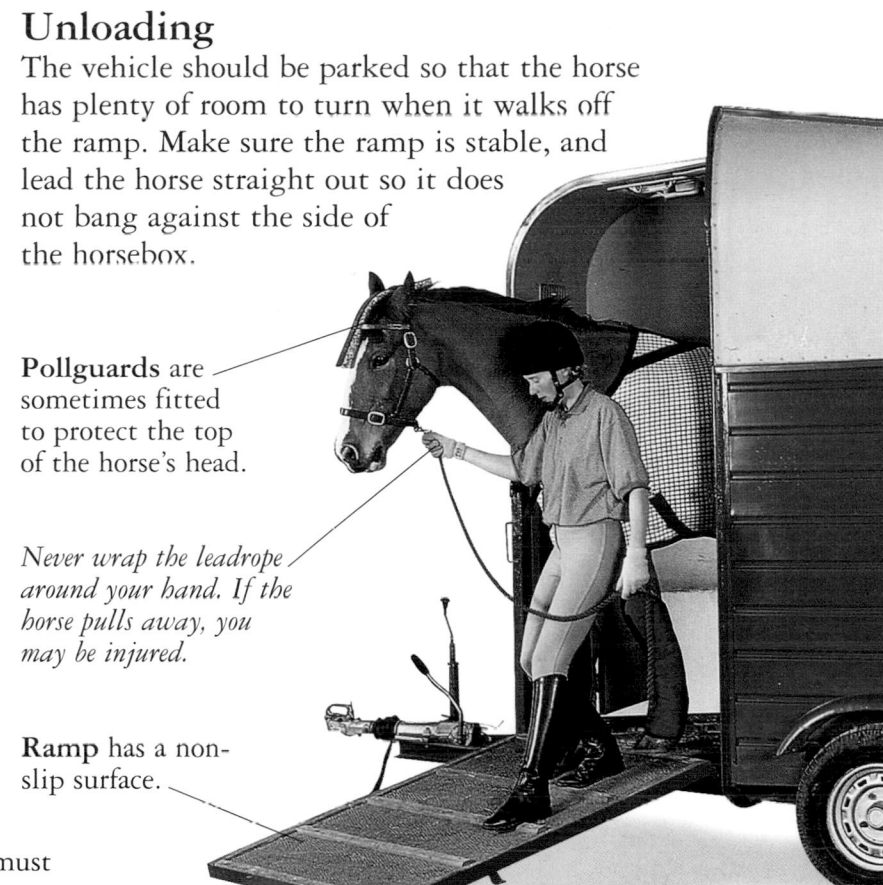

Pollguards are sometimes fitted to protect the top of the horse's head.

Never wrap the leadrope around your hand. If the horse pulls away, you may be injured.

Ramp has a non-slip surface.

Roof height must allow sufficient headroom for the horse.

Wear a hard hat when loading unknown or unpredictable horses.

Always fit a travelling horse with a suitable rug.

Tail bandage or tailguard protects tail hair from rubbing.

Travel boots or bandages prevent leg injuries.

SAFETY

YOUR HORSE'S SAFETY depends on you, so check the field and stable yard every day to make sure they are clean and safe, thus helping to prevent illness or injury. It is also important to care for your own safety by handling horses correctly and never taking risks – even quiet horses may be unpredictable if they are ill or frightened. First-aid kits for both horses and people should always be available.

First aid for riders

Every stable yard should have first-aid kits for riders. Your doctor can advise you on what to include in a first-aid kit. A telephone should also be available, with emergency numbers displayed.

First-aid kit includes bandages, dressings, and scissors.

Safety at the stable yard

The buildings and stables in a yard must be kept in good repair, and tools and equipment should be stored safely when not in use. Dogs and young children should be supervised and not allowed to run around.

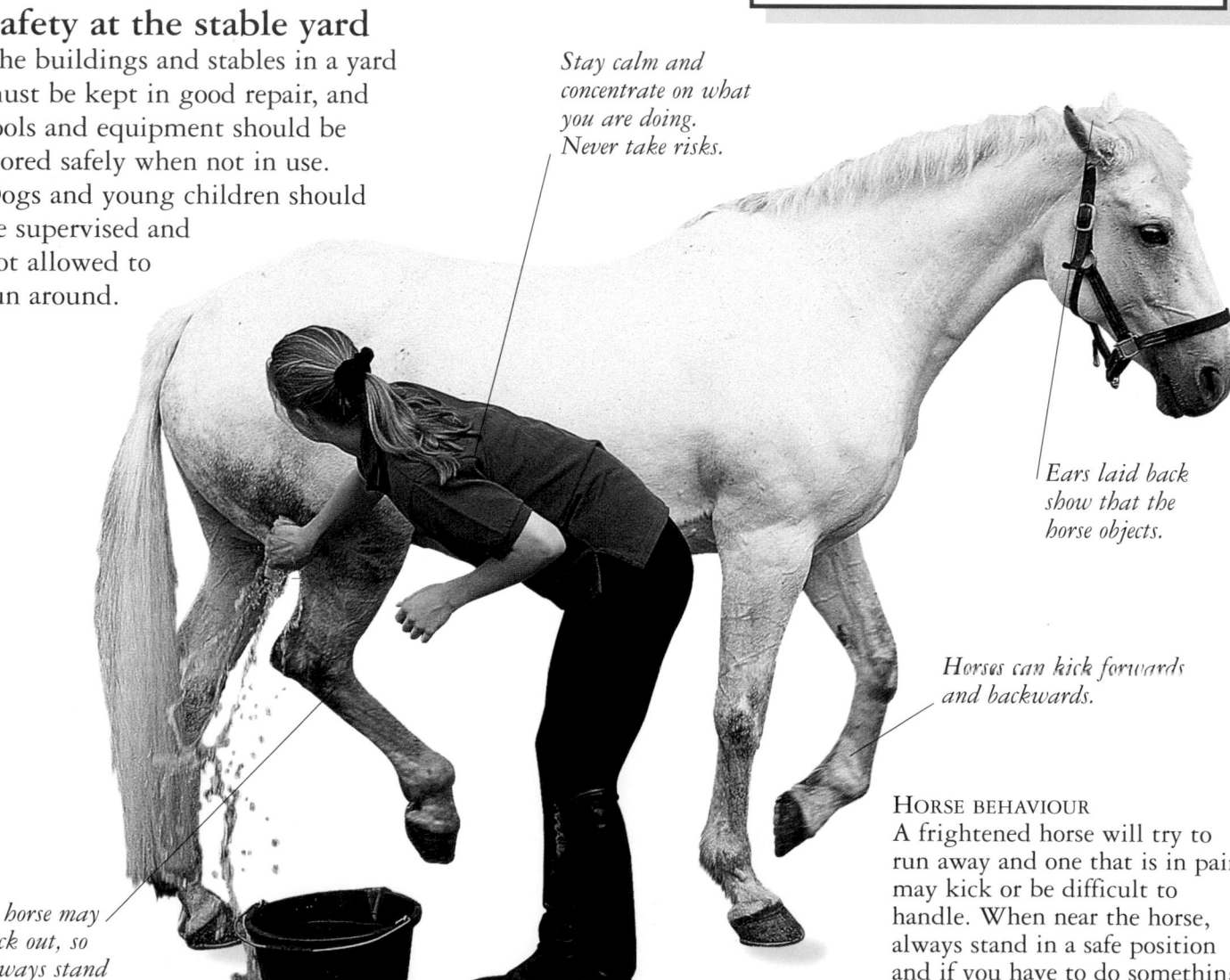

Stay calm and concentrate on what you are doing. Never take risks.

Ears laid back show that the horse objects.

Horses can kick forwards and backwards.

A horse may kick out, so always stand to one side of it.

HORSE BEHAVIOUR

A frightened horse will try to run away and one that is in pain may kick or be difficult to handle. When near the horse, always stand in a safe position and if you have to do something the horse may object to, tie it up. If necessary, ask for help.

KEEPING YOUR HORSE SAFE

Daily checks to the field and fencing, and careful stable management will help you create a safe environment for your horse. By carrying out these checks you will minimize the risks of injury to your horse of both illness and injury, for example from broken fencing. It is also important to take precautions against theft and fire.

IN THE STABLE

STABLE MANAGEMENT
Keep the stable clean and dust-free. Provide the horse with a deep bed, so that it doesn't injure itself on the stable floor. Disinfect the floor and walls at least twice a year. Wash buckets every day.

SECURITY
Protect your horse from theft by using a security marking system such as freeze marking. Mark tack and equipment with your postcode or address. Keep your horse where someone can keep an eye on it.

FIRE PRECAUTIONS
Keep a fire extinguisher and hosepipe in clear view so that everyone can see where they are kept. Make sure electricity supplies are safe and kept away from water sources.

KEEPING STABLE IN GOOD REPAIR
Stables should be kept in good repair so that there are no visible nails, broken wood, or other sharp objects that could injure a horse. Doors should have fastenings at top and bottom, so that they can be shut tight when the horse is in the stable.

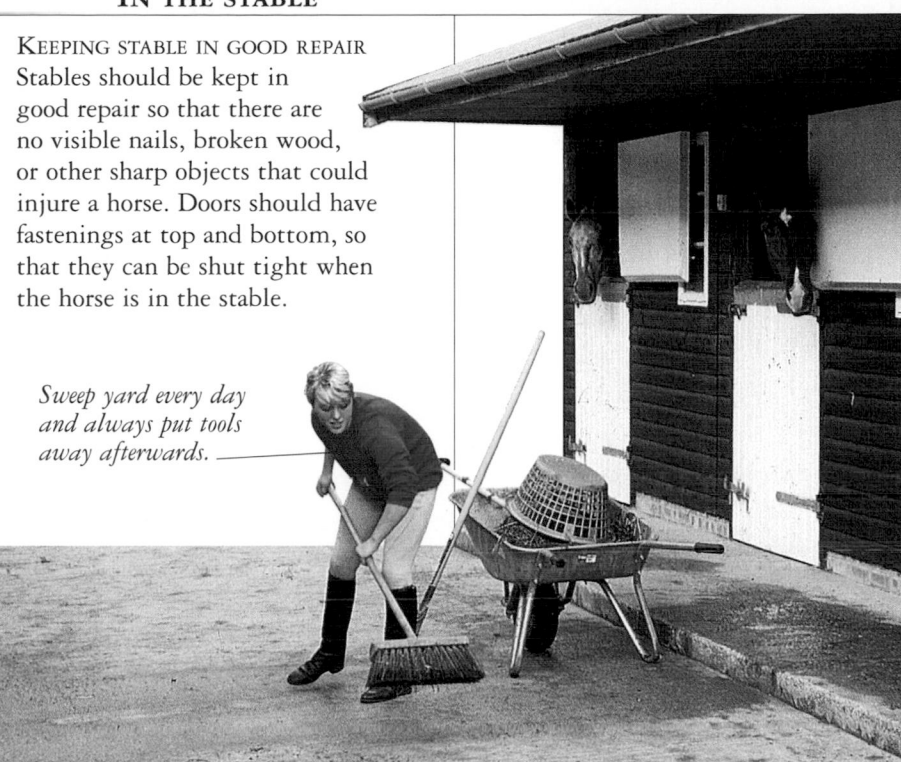

Sweep yard every day and always put tools away afterwards.

AT GRASS

Always provide clean water

CHECKING WATER SUPPLY
Use a container that horses cannot knock over to provide a constant supply of clean water. These should not have any sharp edges or projections that could injure a horse. Keep container free from debris, such as fallen leaves, and if necessary, break any frozen ice.

FILLING IN HOLES
Use spare soil to fill in holes in the field made by rabbits, moles, or other animals. If a horse puts its foot down a hole it could break its leg. If your field has a lot of holes, get expert advice on pest control.

KEEPING THE FIELD CLEAN
Remove droppings from the field as often as possible, preferably every day. This helps to reduce the amount of worm eggs that live in horse droppings, thus lessening health risks to the horse. Get advice on harrowing large fields.

REMOVING POISONOUS PLANTS
Learn to identify poisonous plants such as ragwort, yew, and deadly nightshade. Remove and burn them. Acorns are poisonous, so fence off oak trees and their surroundings.

CHECKING FENCING
Check fencing daily for weak or broken parts. Electric fencing must be correctly installed; check that nothing is touching the electrified parts, thus causing a short circuit. If you are unsure, ask an expert how to use electric fencing.

HORSE CARE

ROUTINE CARE, such as grooming, is the
responsibility of those looking after a horse or pony –
usually you. Other tasks, such as vaccinating, must
be done by qualified professionals. Never forget preventative
measures such as worming, or your horse's health will suffer.

JOB	DESCRIPTION
SIGNS OF ILL HEALTH	Always be alert for signs that a horse may be ill or injured. Danger signs include heat or swelling in the legs, restlessness and sweating, eye or nasal discharge, laboured breathing, and listlessness.
WORMING	Worming is the administration of paste from syringes directly into a horse's mouth, or putting granules into the feed. The vet will advise you on which products to use.
VACCINATE	All horses should be vaccinated against tetanus and equine influenza. Breeding animals may need extra vaccinations, so check with the vet.
SHOEING	All horses should have their feet trimmed regularly to prevent them growing too long. Most horses need to wear shoes when working on hard ground.
RASP TEETH	Sharp teeth and hooks (curved projections on a tooth) are rasped down using special dental equipment.
CHECK FIELD	Check the field for broken or weak fencing and repair when needed. Remove and burn poisonous plants, and any rubbish. Fill in holes made by small animals. Remove droppings.
GROOMING	Stabled horses need to be groomed thoroughly. Grass-kept horses need coat grease for protection, so just brush off dried mud and tidy mane and tail.
CLIPPING	This is the removal of all, or parts, of a horse's winter coat, using special electric or battery operated equine clippers.
TACK FIT	Check that the bit, bridle, and saddle are the correct size and tack is not damaged or faulty.

Trotting up horse to observe its action.

Feeding a pony

Rugs need to be put on horses that are clipped or have thin winter coats. A sick horse will need rugs to keep it warm. Take off and replace rugs at least once a day.

PUTTING ON A RUG

MUCKING OUT TOOLS

Mucking out every day keeps a horse's stable free from harmful gases given off by wet, dirty bedding. Store tools safely after use.

FREQUENCY	WHO DOES IT	WHY
Each time you see the pony, especially first thing in the morning.	You or anyone else responsible for the horse's care.	The sooner potential problems are spotted, the more likely it is that the horse will make a quick recovery. In colic cases, speedy action can save a horse's life.
Every six to eight weeks on veterinary advice.	You – ask someone to show you how to administer paste.	All horses have some worms in their intestines. Worming reduces the amount of worms in the body to a safe level.
A primary course is followed by annual boosters.	Vet	To protect horses against conditions that can, at times, be fatal.
Every four to six weeks.	A farrier. In the UK only a registered farrier can shoe horses.	Domestic horses' hooves do not wear down fast enough, unlike those of wild horses, which are constantly on the move.
Once or twice a year, depending on needs of individual horse.	Vet or trained equine dentist.	Rasping teeth helps to keep a horse comfortable when it is wearing a bit. It also improves a horse's ability to chew and digest food.
Every day	You or anyone else responsible for the horse's care.	Check the field to stop horse from escaping and to prevent injury or illness. Removing droppings helps reduce amount of worms.
Every day	You or anyone else responsible for the horse's care.	Helps keep coat and skin healthy and helps you spot wounds, heat, or swelling.
Up to three times a year once horse's winter coat is fully grown.	Must be done by an experienced adult.	Enables horse to work without sweating too much.
Check for safety every time you ride. Check saddle fit every month.	Always get expert advice, especially for saddles and bits.	Badly fitting tack can cause discomfort, injury, and poor performance.

Cleaning the nose

HORSE & PONY BREEDS

ORIGINS

THERE ARE MORE than 75 breeds of horses and ponies. All can be traced back to the same ancestors that appeared on Earth c.55 million years ago. By the time the horse was domesticated about 6,000 years ago, there were four types of horses. From these types developed certain breeds such as the Arab, which have had a great impact on the development of modern horses.

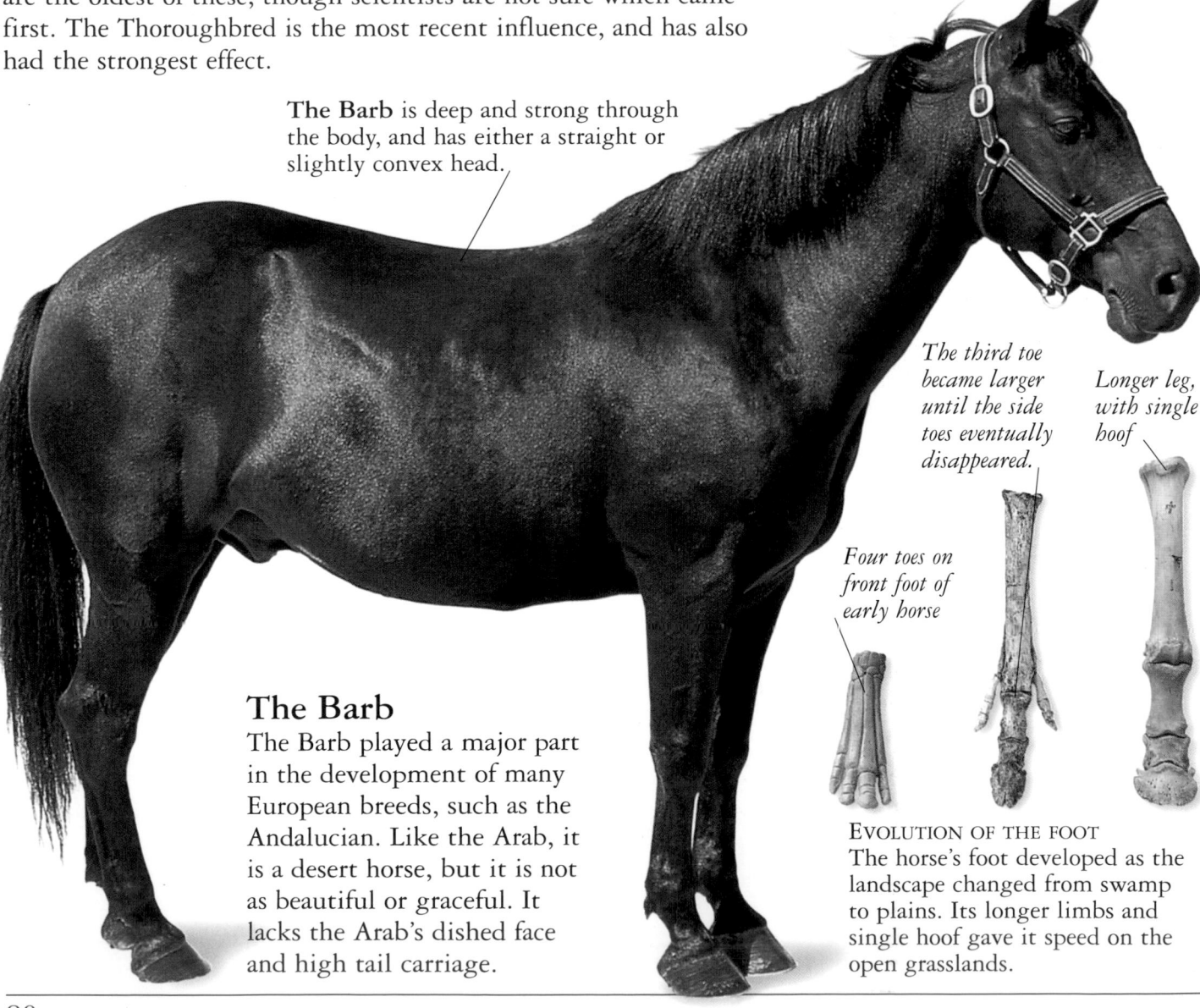

THE FIRST HORSE
Eohippus, or the Dawn Horse, was about 36 cm (14 in) high. It had four toes on each front foot, and three on the hind foot. *Eohippus* fed on leaves, since there was no grass.

The greatest influences

The three main influences on modern riding horses and ponies are the Arab, the Barb, and the Thoroughbred. The Arab and the Barb are the oldest of these, though scientists are not sure which came first. The Thoroughbred is the most recent influence, and has also had the strongest effect.

The Barb is deep and strong through the body, and has either a straight or slightly convex head.

The third toe became larger until the side toes eventually disappeared.

Longer leg, with single hoof

Four toes on front foot of early horse

The Barb

The Barb played a major part in the development of many European breeds, such as the Andalucian. Like the Arab, it is a desert horse, but it is not as beautiful or graceful. It lacks the Arab's dished face and high tail carriage.

EVOLUTION OF THE FOOT
The horse's foot developed as the landscape changed from swamp to plains. Its longer limbs and single hoof gave it speed on the open grasslands.

Dense coat protects against cold and wet.

EXMOOR

Heavy build helps to cope with cold and frost.

Coarser limbs and feathers

HIGHLAND

Thin neck is set very high and supports head with fine ears.

This type had a long, narrow body and was lean and thin-skinned.

AKHAL-TEKE

Refined build and slim body

Dished head, characteristics of both the Arab and Caspian pony

CASPIAN

Pony type 1

Found in north-west Europe, this pony type was about 12.2 hh. It had a straight profile and small ears. This hardy pony was highly resistant to wet and able to thrive in harsh conditions. The Exmoor pony is its nearest modern equivalent.

Pony type 2

Standing at about 14.2 hh, this type was heavily built and coarse in appearance. Its head was large in relation to its body. This pony settled in northern Eurasia, where it was able to survive the cold. The Highland pony is its nearest equivalent.

Horse type 3

A horse rather than a pony, this horse type stood at about 15 hh. It had a long body, long neck, and long ears and was shallow through the girth. Living in central Asia, it was resistant to heat and drought. The Akhal-Teke is the modern breed that resembles it most closely.

Horse type 4

This type was a pony in terms of height, but a miniature horse in terms of conformation. It had a "dished" face and a high tail carriage. A dished face is a characteristic of both the Arab and Caspian pony; some scientists believe that horse type 4 was the blueprint for these breeds.

THE MODERN HORSE

MODERN HORSES and ponies are bred for specific functions. These range from pleasure riding, driving, and working on the land, to competing in specialist sports such as dressage, racing, and showjumping. Horses can be classified by breed, type, colour, and markings. A horse bred for one type of activity may not be suitable for another. Some, however, are adaptable and have many uses.

Warmbloods

Warmbloods are the ultimate modern sports horses. They combine Thoroughbred, or hot blood, with cold blood, or heavier horse, influences. Warmbloods are the result of careful breeding programmes.

Performance horses are used to breed warmbloods.

Classification of the horse

The two main types of horse are heavy and light. Ponies form a third group. Heavy horses include the largest, most powerful breeds, and often stand at more than 17 hh. Light horse breeds and types, such as riding horses, stand at more than 14.2 hh, while ponies stand at 14.2 hh or less.

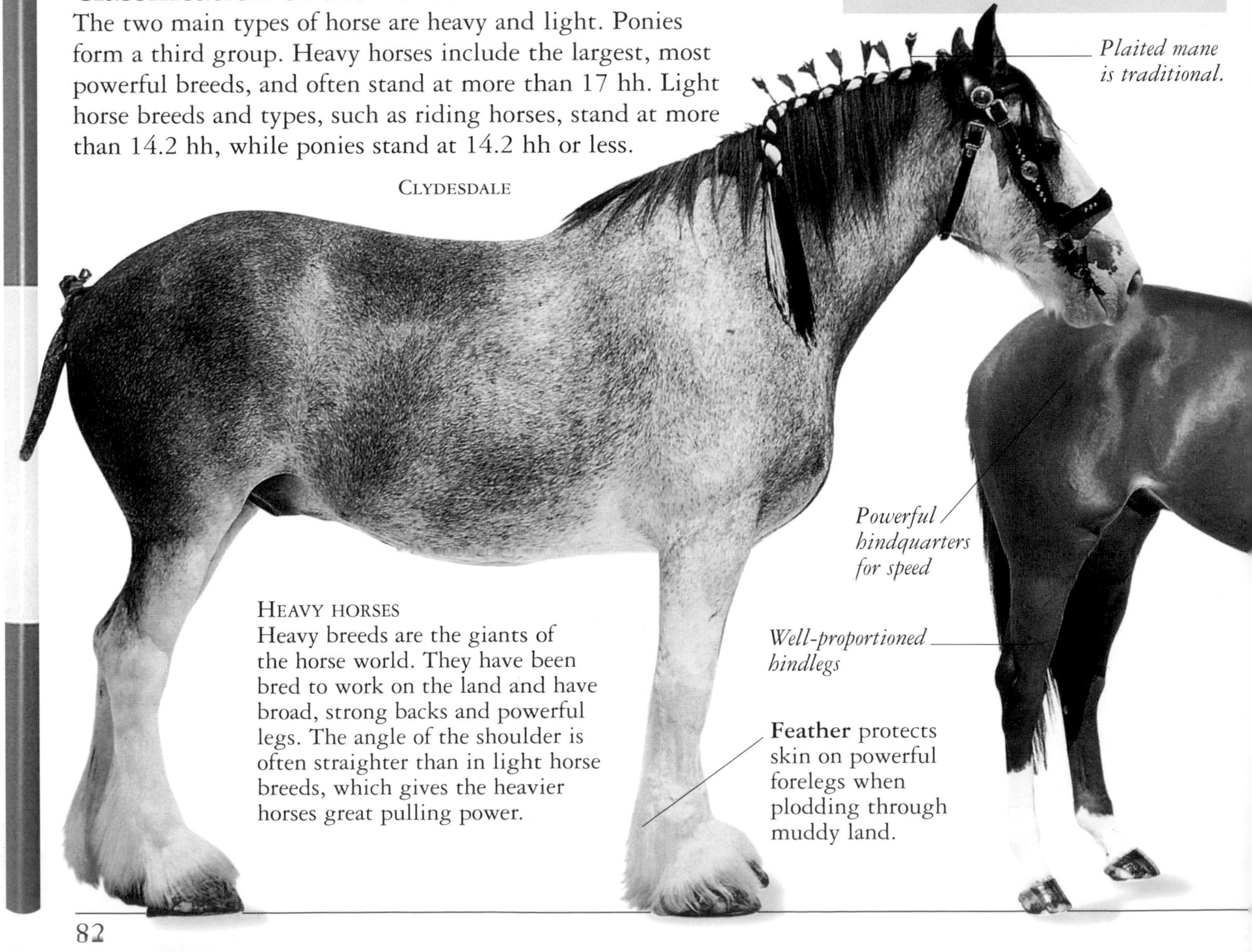

CLYDESDALE

Plaited mane is traditional.

Powerful hindquarters for speed

Well-proportioned hindlegs

HEAVY HORSES
Heavy breeds are the giants of the horse world. They have been bred to work on the land and have broad, strong backs and powerful legs. The angle of the shoulder is often straighter than in light horse breeds, which gives the heavier horses great pulling power.

Feather protects skin on powerful forelegs when plodding through muddy land.

COLOURS AND MARKINGS

Colours and markings are key identification points for horses and ponies. Colours can be solid or broken, and some horses, such as palominos, are bred specifically for their colour. Face and leg markings are white patches on a solid colour, such as chestnut.

COLOURS

COAT COLOURINGS

Colour is determined by the horse's genetic make-up. Some colours are always dominant. For example, if one parent is grey and the other is either bay, black, or chestnut, the foal will always be grey. There are also classifications within the colours, so a skewbald may be called a tobiano or an overo depending on the distribution of solid colour compared to white.

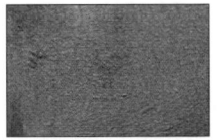

DUN   PALOMINO   PIEBALD   SPOTTED

CHESTNUT   SKEWBALD   BAY   DAPPLE GREY

MARKINGS

FACE AND LEG MARKINGS

The most common face markings are stars, stripes, snips, or combinations of these. A white or bald face covers the forehead and front of the face. Leg markings include socks, which extend up to the knees, while stockings run further up the leg.

  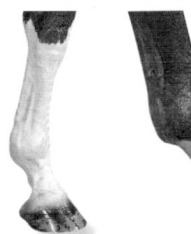  

STRIPE   STAR   STOCKING   SOCK   ERMINE

THOROUGHBRED

Fine coat and slender build help horse to stay cool.

Bushy mane protects pony against cold and wet weather.

WELSH PONY

Long, sloping shoulder indicates good movement and a comfortable ride.

Body is compact with depth through the girth.

LIGHT HORSE

The light horse riding breeds and types always have some Thoroughbred blood. Their body shape and movement makes them comfortable to ride.

PONY

Different pony breeds have height restrictions and definite characteristics depending on the type of work for which they were traditionally used. Many are tough and hardy.

Short forearms help bear weight.

PHYSICAL FEATURES

THE HORSE HAS acute senses, which, together with its physical characteristics and shape, enable it to spot potential dangers and flee. Correct conformation, or shape, is not just important because it makes the horse beautiful; if the horse's body and legs have the right proportions and angles, it will be more likely to stay sound and be athletic. No horse is perfect, but its strengths should outweigh its weaknesses.

Conformation

A well-made horse has good hooves and legs to support its body easily. Its back, quarters, and hindlegs should be strong, and its body deep for efficient heart and lung function. A sloping shoulder angle helps the riding horse move gracefully.

Strong loins and back give strength. The back must not be too long or too short.

Powerful hindquarters are needed for propulsion.

Hocks that are correctly angled provide the hindlegs with power.

Well-proportioned hindlegs

Hooves should not be broken or split.

How to measure a horse

Stand a horse on level ground so that its hooves are square and its head and neck are at a natural angle. Measure from the highest part of the withers down to the ground. Horses are traditionally measured in hands and inches.

A hand is 10 cm (4 in).

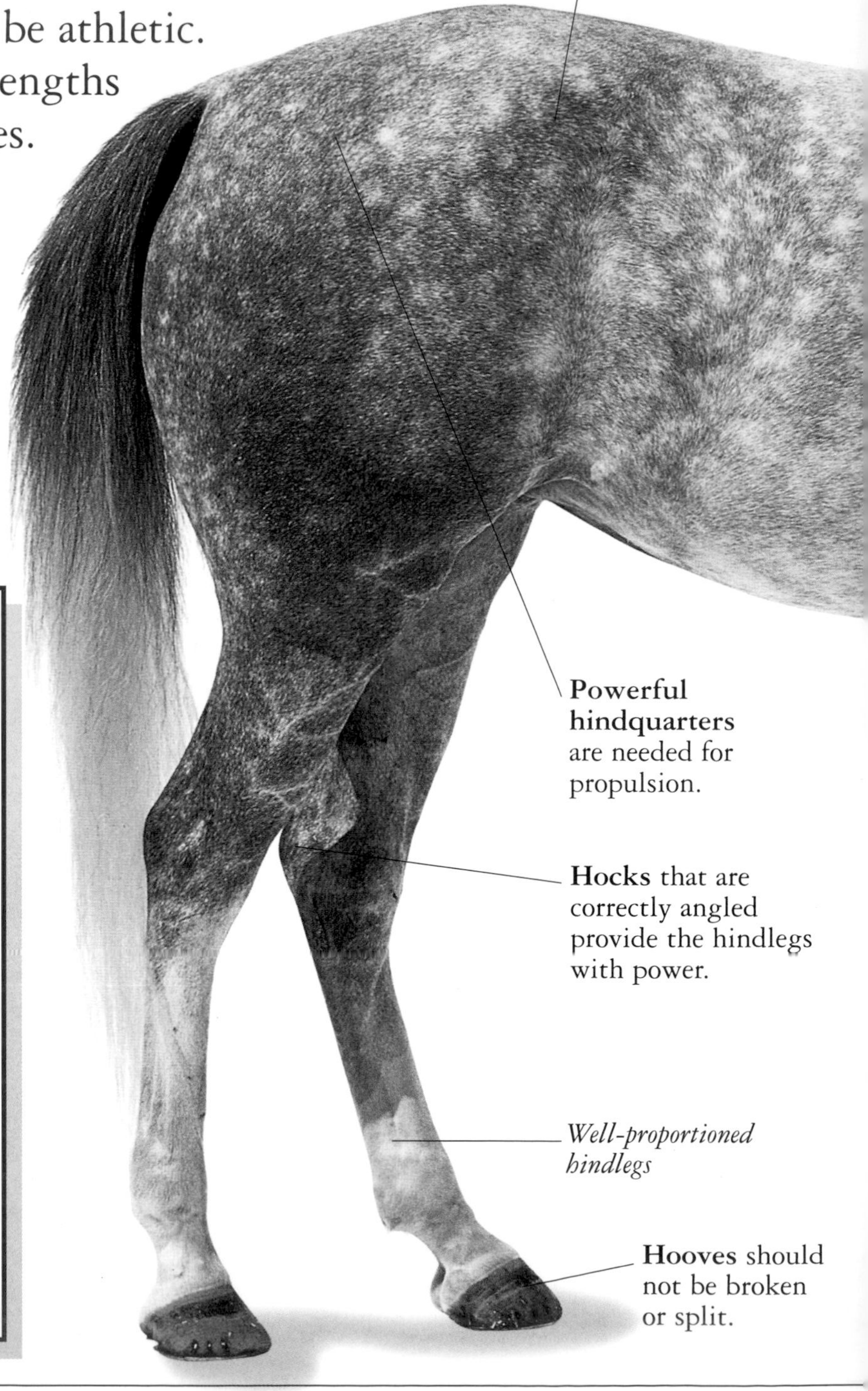

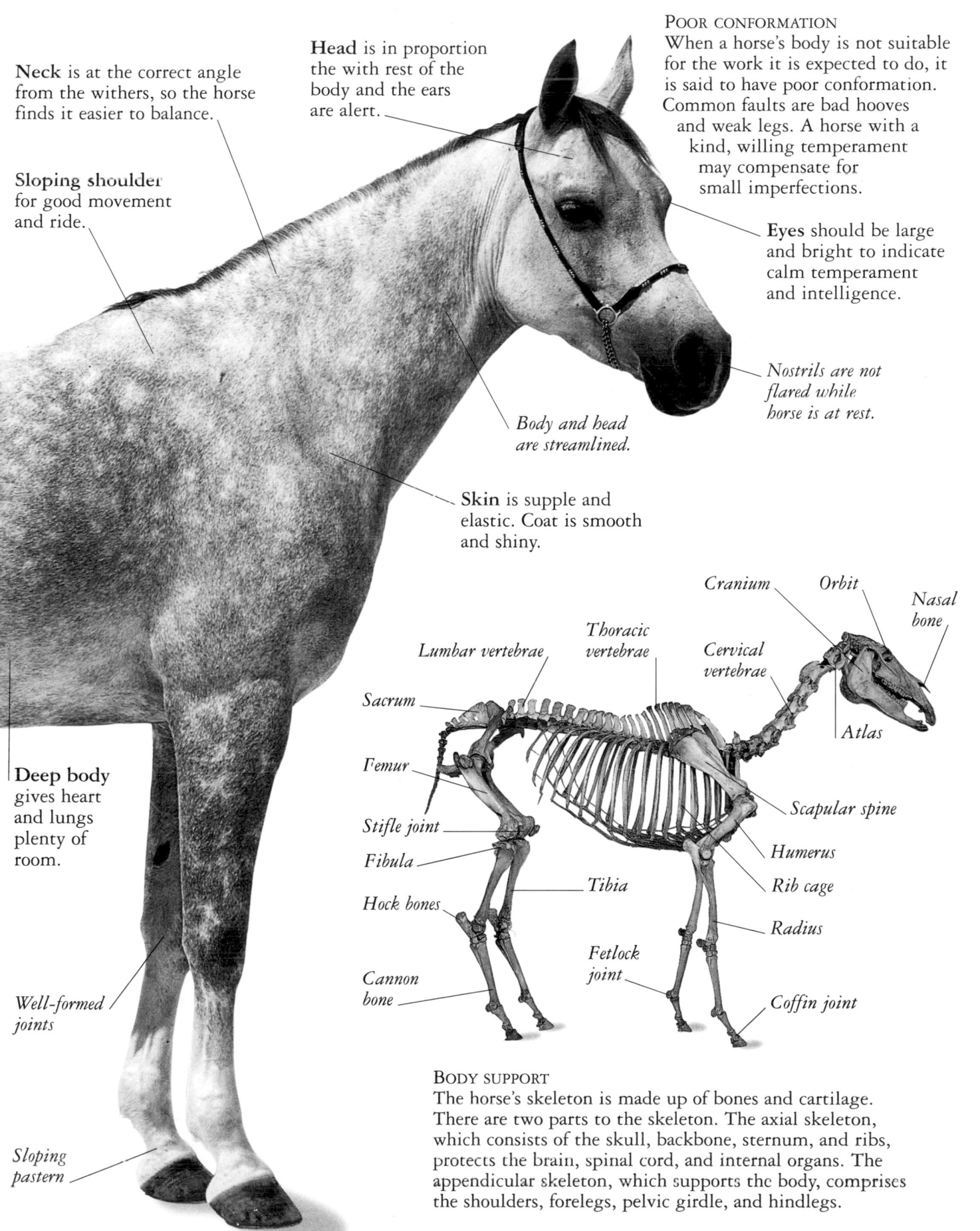

Neck is at the correct angle from the withers, so the horse finds it easier to balance.

Head is in proportion the with rest of the body and the ears are alert.

POOR CONFORMATION
When a horse's body is not suitable for the work it is expected to do, it is said to have poor conformation. Common faults are bad hooves and weak legs. A horse with a kind, willing temperament may compensate for small imperfections.

Sloping shoulder for good movement and ride.

Eyes should be large and bright to indicate calm temperament and intelligence.

Nostrils are not flared while horse is at rest.

Body and head are streamlined.

Skin is supple and elastic. Coat is smooth and shiny.

Cranium   *Orbit*

Nasal bone

Thoracic vertebrae

Lumbar vertebrae   *Cervical vertebrae*

Sacrum

Atlas

Femur

Scapular spine

Stifle joint

Humerus

Fibula

Rib cage

Tibia

Radius

Hock bones

Fetlock joint

Coffin joint

Deep body gives heart and lungs plenty of room.

Cannon bone

Well-formed joints

BODY SUPPORT
The horse's skeleton is made up of bones and cartilage. There are two parts to the skeleton. The axial skeleton, which consists of the skull, backbone, sternum, and ribs, protects the brain, spinal cord, and internal organs. The appendicular skeleton, which supports the body, comprises the shoulders, forelegs, pelvic girdle, and hindlegs.

Sloping pastern

HORSE AND PONY TYPES

HORSES CAN BE classified by type as well as breed. Sometimes a horse's breeding is unspecific, but its conformation, build, and movement make it a particular type. Types have a set of physical characteristics that help them perform specific functions, such as hunting, hacking, or farming. However, some breeds have a powerful influence on types. For example, Thoroughbred blood gives quality and extra agility to riding and sport horses, while most cobs have some draught horse ancestry.

Different types

Some horses such as cobs, hunters, and hacks, fulfil a particular purpose, but do not belong to a specific breed. When horses of the same type breed, their offspring will often, but not always, have the same characteristics.

Domestic horses

For many centuries, all horses were wild. They were not domesticated until about 6,000 years ago. Today, although the Camargue horses of southern France live in the wild, they are kept in herds and used to work the area's black cattle. The only truly wild horse is Przewalski's horse.

A calm temperament is essential for riding horses.

RIDING HORSE
The ideal riding horse is a perfectly proportioned light horse. It usually has at least 50 per cent Thoroughbred.

Hindlegs are fine, but strong

Feather is clipped off riding cobs.

Hooves are good-sized for working on rough ground.

COB
The cob is a deep-bodied horse with short legs. It has a great weight-carrying ability and was originally used by farmers. Show cobs must be more than 14.2 hh, but must not exceed 15.1 hh.

Fairly long, well-muscled neck is important for balance.

Elegant frame is combined with a fine coat.

Long forearms for good movement and strength.

Hindlegs and hindquarters are powerful for quick turns and acceleration.

Joints and legs that are clean and strong enable horse to run far and fast.

POLO PONY
Horses used for polo are always called ponies. Most are between 15 hh and 15.3 hh. Thoroughbreds crossed with Argentinian Criollo ponies are popular breeds for polo.

THOROUGHBRED
Although not strictly a type, the Thoroughbred has more influence than any other breed on the modern types of horse. It is the fastest of the breeds and gives physical quality to any breed or type with which it is crossed.

Mane traditionally clipped

A short, powerful neck supports a noble head.

Hunters must be fit and strong.

Well-sloped shoulders are perfect for galloping and jumping.

Short, strong forelegs carry weight.

HUNTER
The hunter is a powerful horse, that is able to gallop and jump well. It is often a combination of Thoroughbred and draught horse, such as the Irish Draught.

Joints act as shock absorbers.

Forelegs take the strain when jumping and galloping.

THE ARAB

THE ARAB is one of the oldest breeds and is often described as the most beautiful horse in the world. It is easily recognized by its short, refined head and high tail carriage. When crossed with other breeds, these characteristics are often passed on, though to a lesser extent. Tough, hardy, and fast, the Arab excels in racing and endurance sports. It is sensitive and intelligent.

Legends and history

The Arab can be traced back 3,000 years, although legend says it was created by Allah from handfuls of the north and south winds. Bedouin tribesmen allowed their favourite Arab mares to live in their tents. Artists have always been captivated by the Arab's beauty.

Arab versatility

Arabs are hardy and athletic horses with naturally good balance. They are not fashionable for dressage because of their high head and tail carriage, but can perform difficult movements as well as any other breed. Their long stride, great speed, and tough hooves make them naturally good at endurance sports.

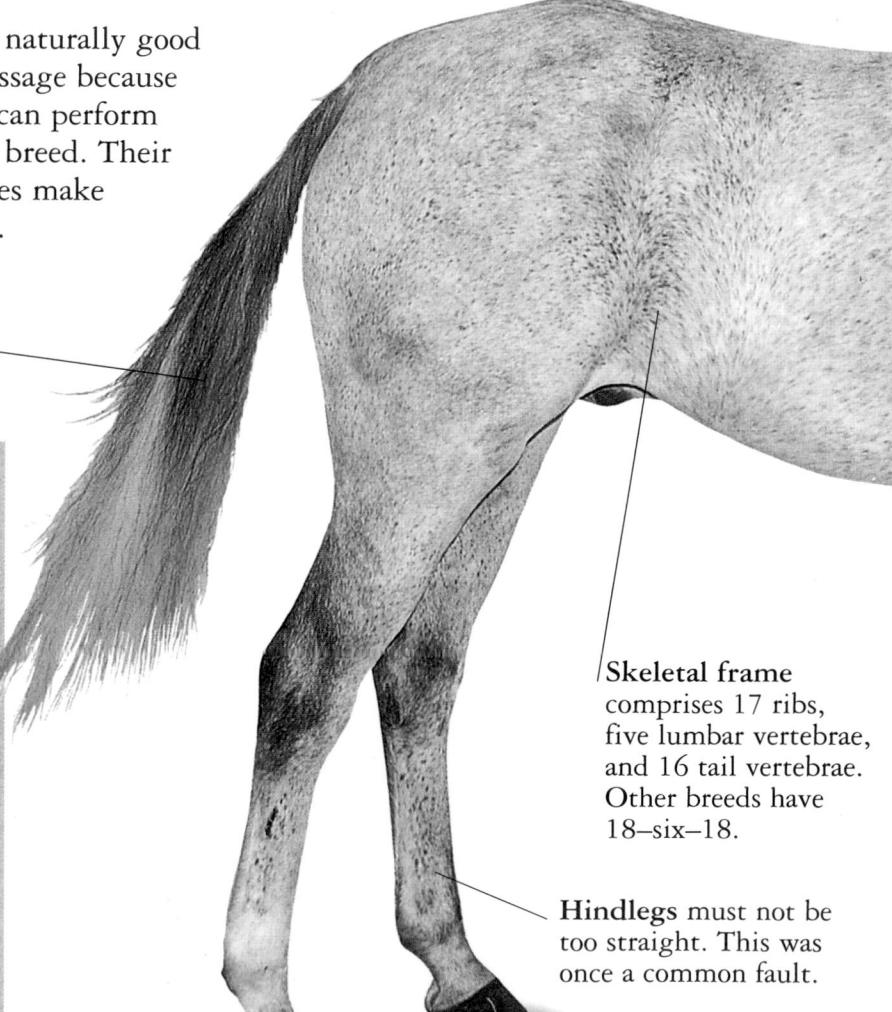

High-set tail

THE ARAB

- Seventeen ribs compared to 18 in other breeds, so it is short-backed

- Bone is denser and stronger than in other breeds

- Mane and tail hair is fine and very silky

- Colours are grey, bay, chestnut, and black

- Muzzle is small with large, flared nostrils

- Legs are long and slender

Skeletal frame comprises 17 ribs, five lumbar vertebrae, and 16 tail vertebrae. Other breeds have 18–six–18.

Hindlegs must not be too straight. This was once a common fault.

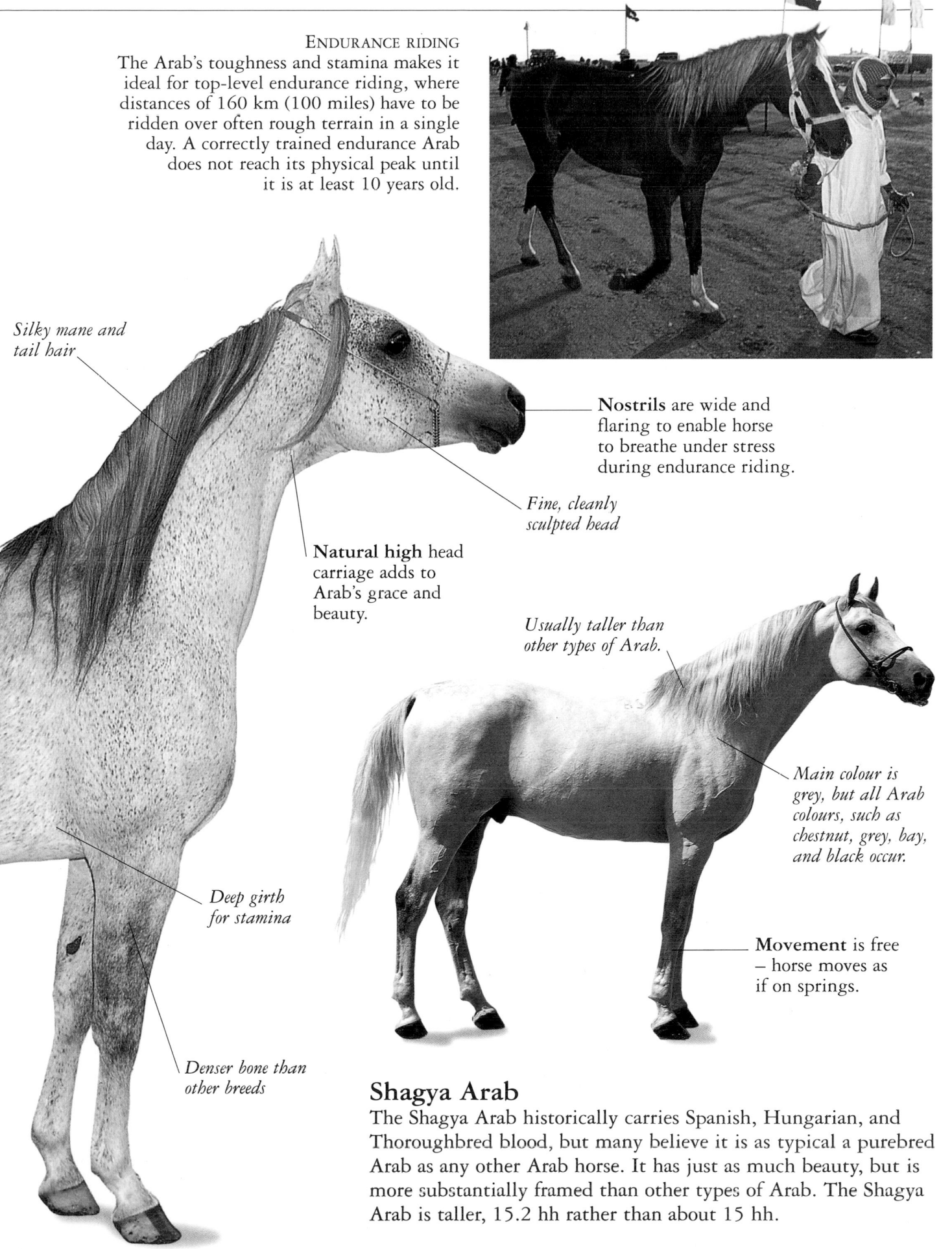

The Arab's toughness and stamina makes it ideal for top-level endurance riding, where distances of 160 km (100 miles) have to be ridden over often rough terrain in a single day. A correctly trained endurance Arab does not reach its physical peak until it is at least 10 years old.

Silky mane and tail hair

Nostrils are wide and flaring to enable horse to breathe under stress during endurance riding.

Fine, cleanly sculpted head

Natural high head carriage adds to Arab's grace and beauty.

Usually taller than other types of Arab.

Main colour is grey, but all Arab colours, such as chestnut, grey, bay, and black occur.

Deep girth for stamina

Movement is free – horse moves as if on springs.

Denser bone than other breeds

Shagya Arab
The Shagya Arab historically carries Spanish, Hungarian, and Thoroughbred blood, but many believe it is as typical a purebred Arab as any other Arab horse. It has just as much beauty, but is more substantially framed than other types of Arab. The Shagya Arab is taller, 15.2 hh rather than about 15 hh.

SPANISH HORSES

THE ANDALUCIAN, which has been known for centuries as the Spanish horse, is the third greatest influence on modern horse and pony breeds. Its beauty and power, combined with a bold but willing temperament, have made it the mount of bullfighters, classical dressage riders, and enthusiasts throughout the world. The Lusitano and the Lipizzaner also have strong Spanish influences.

HARNESS CHAMPIONS
The Andalucian, Lusitano, and Lipizzaner are all spectacular carriage horses and are also highly prized as riding horses. Their good movement is combined with a trainable temperament.

The Andalucian

The Andalucian is a powerful horse with a substantial frame that makes it look bigger than its average 15.2 hh. Its movement is controlled and high stepping. Strong hindquarters give it a natural ability for advanced dressage movements.

Hindquarters are particularly strong.

Coat colour is usually grey or bay.

Powerful hock joints add strength.

Knee joints should be large and flat for soundness and toughness.

Tail is long, luxurious, and often wavy.

SPANISH HORSES

- Once unfashionable, these breeds are now finding favour with some dressage riders

- All three breeds are usually grey

- Kind temperament means that stallions are favoured for riding

- Mares are traditionally used only for breeding

- The Alter Real is a breed that also descends from Andalucian stock

The Lipizzaner

The Lipizzaner is most famous as the dancing white horse of the Spanish Riding School in Vienna. During the war in Bosnia and Croatia in the 1990s, Lipizzaners at the former State Stud in Bosnia were saved by an international rescue operation, thus preserving valuable bloodlines. The horses have been bred at this stud for 400 years.

Horses at the Spanish Riding School are all Lipizzaner stallions.

Lipizzaners are grey, but are dark when born.

The levade is one of the movements performed by the talented Spanish Riding School horses.

Spanish Riding School's riders are all men who must reach a high standard on schooled stallions before being allowed to train young ones.

Powerful, crested neck with silky and often wavy mane.

Handsome, straight profile

Short back and good loin

Profile is straight like that of the Andalucian.

Brand denotes bloodlines and stud of origin.

Coat can come in all colours but is mainly grey.

The Lusitano

The Portuguese Lusitano, developed from the Andalucian, has a slight Arab influence, but is longer and lighter in the limbs. Highly-schooled Lusitanos are ridden by Portuguese bullfighters, called "rejoneadores".

Cannon bone is particularly long.

THOROUGHBRED

THE THOROUGHBRED EVOLVED during the 17th and 18th centuries. It is the fastest and most valuable breed in the world, and is often crossed with other breeds to improve their quality. Thoroughbreds are generally bred for racing, but are also successful in horse trials and other sports.

Anglo-arab

The Anglo-arab is a cross between the two most influential breeds in the world, the Thoroughbred and the Arab. It looks like the Thoroughbred in appearance, but ideally it should combine the speed of the Thoroughbred with the toughness of the Arab, and share the beauty of both.

Thoroughbred

The Thoroughbred has had a strong influence on all breeds of modern sport horse. The best have great courage, mental stamina, and speed. They can be highly strung and usually have sharp reactions.

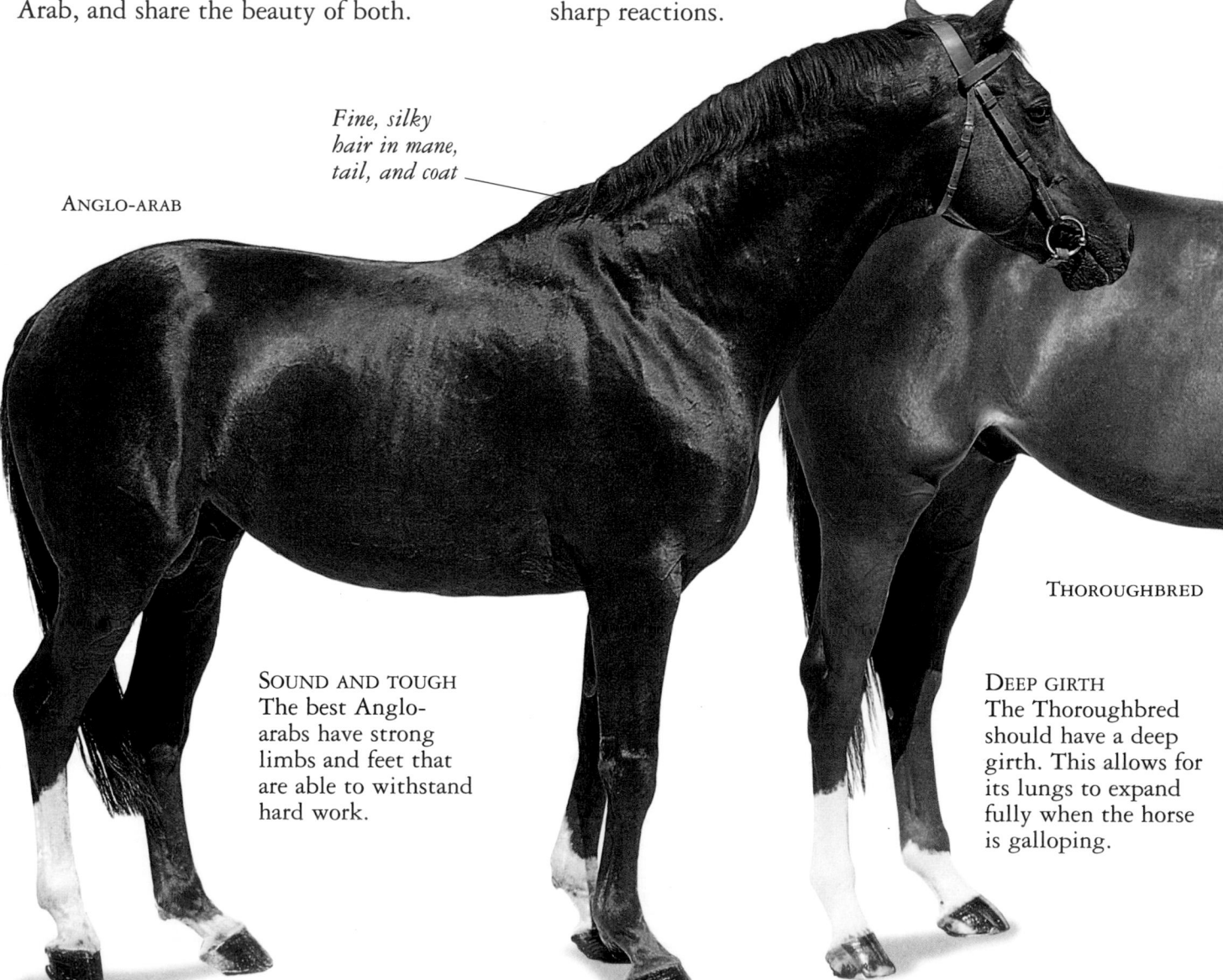

Fine, silky hair in mane, tail, and coat

ANGLO-ARAB

THOROUGHBRED

SOUND AND TOUGH
The best Anglo-arabs have strong limbs and feet that are able to withstand hard work.

DEEP GIRTH
The Thoroughbred should have a deep girth. This allows for its lungs to expand fully when the horse is galloping.

Born to race

The Thoroughbred is built for speed. There are two different types. Flat racehorses are usually more finely built and race as two and three-year-olds. Steeplechasers race over fences and do not start until they are four years old. Their racing careers last much longer than flat racehorses, sometimes until they are about 13 years old.

American standardbred

The Standardbred is America's own racing breed. Its breeding has Thoroughbred influence from the 18th century. It is a harness racing horse that pulls a special lightweight vehicle, usually over distances of 1.6 km (one mile). The breed's name comes from the 19th century, when horses had to meet a standard time in races to enter the breed register.

Lower-set neck can be stretched out in a racing finish.

POWERFUL QUARTERS
The Standardbred's croup is usually higher than its withers. This gives powerful thrust to the quarters, making the horse a successful harness racer.

Colours are mainly bay, as here, brown, black, and chestnut.

Strong limbs reduce the risk of injury when the horse is racing at speed.

AMERICAN STANDARDBRED

MOUNTAIN AND MOORLAND PONIES

MOUNTAIN AND MOORLAND ponies are able to survive harsh living conditions. They first came from the British Isles, where they are native ponies, but are now bred all over the world. They can carry heavy weights for their size, and the larger breeds can be ridden by adults or children. They are often crossed with Thoroughbreds to produce sport horses.

Moorland ponies
The Exmoor is a rare breed. It has a fan of hair at the top of the tail, called an ice tail, which protects it from bad weather. Another moorland pony, the Dartmoor pony, is more elegant than the Exmoor.

Exmoors are always bay, brown, or dun.

Small breeds
Dartmoor, Exmoor, Shetland, and Welsh A and B ponies are small but strong. Their kind temperaments and athletic abilities make them good to ride if trained correctly. They also make sound driving ponies.

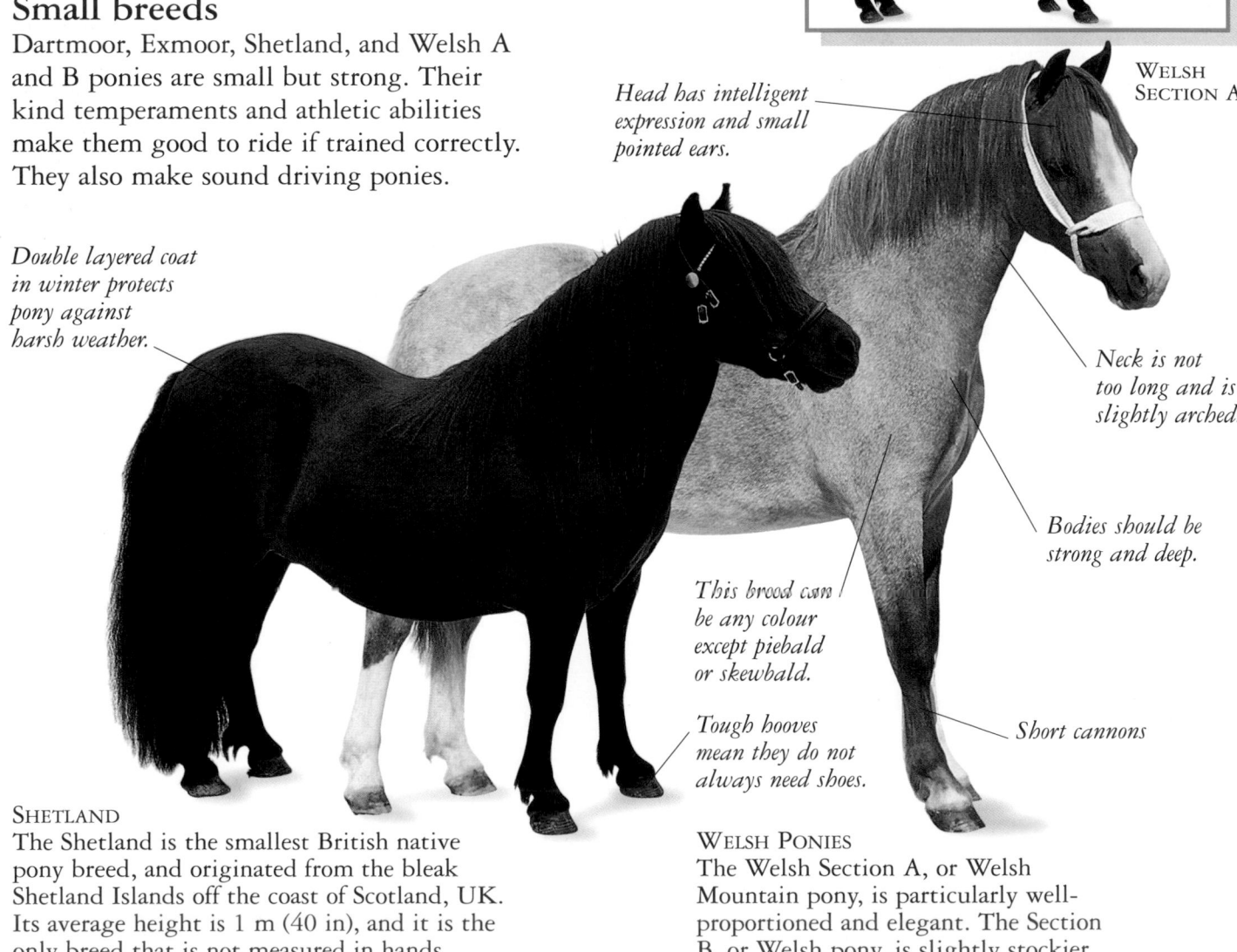

WELSH SECTION A

Head has intelligent expression and small pointed ears.

Double layered coat in winter protects pony against harsh weather.

Neck is not too long and is slightly arched.

Bodies should be strong and deep.

This breed can be any colour except piebald or skewbald.

Tough hooves mean they do not always need shoes.

Short cannons

SHETLAND
The Shetland is the smallest British native pony breed, and originated from the bleak Shetland Islands off the coast of Scotland, UK. Its average height is 1 m (40 in), and it is the only breed that is not measured in hands.

WELSH PONIES
The Welsh Section A, or Welsh Mountain pony, is particularly well-proportioned and elegant. The Section B, or Welsh pony, is slightly stockier.

Large breeds

The larger native breeds are bred as performance ponies for children and adults. The Connemara and Welsh Section D are the most popular and are often good jumpers.

Long neck and good shoulder make a comfortable ride.

Usual colours are bay, brown, and chestnut.

Strong hocks and hindquarters for powerful stride.

Connemara is usually grey, dun, or bay.

NEW FOREST
New Forest ponies have been influenced by the introduction of Welsh and Thoroughbred blood. They are sure-footed and have kind temperaments.

WELSH SECTION D
Also called the Welsh Cob, this pony is the largest British native breed and can be over 15 hh. It often has a powerful trot.

CONNEMARA
Originally bred in Ireland and popular throughout the world, the Connemara has a range of uses from dressage to jumping.

Strong back and hindquarters for carrying weight.

FELL

Tails and manes are uncut.

Coat is usually dun or grey in colour.

Fine, silky feather on lower legs.

FELL AND DALES
The Fell and Dales ponies look similar, although the Fell is slightly smaller and lighter in build. Both are usually black, brown, or bay and have thick, silky leg feather.

HIGHLAND
The Highland pony is very strong and can carry a weight of up to 18 stone (126 kg). It often has a dark stripe, called an eel stripe, down the centre of its back.

EUROPEAN PONIES

EUROPEAN PONIES might not be as well-known worldwide as British native ponies, but their popularity is growing fast. Haflingers and Fjords, in particular, make good riding and driving ponies, and are prized as purebreds rather than as possible crosses with Thoroughbreds. The Haflinger has influenced the Italian Bardigiano, while the Fjord resembles the Highland pony.

Pony power

Many European ponies are kept for work as well as for pleasure. They are usually strong and sturdy, which makes them ideal for harness work in mountainous areas. They also thrive in harsh conditions, and are less expensive to feed than large horses.

Bardigiano

The Bardigiano is an Italian breed of mountain pony. It has been influenced by draught horse blood and by the Avelignese, a pony that is very similar to, but heavier than, the Haflinger.

Coat is often bay or brown, with no white markings.

Mane is cut to stand on end, so the black centre shows through.

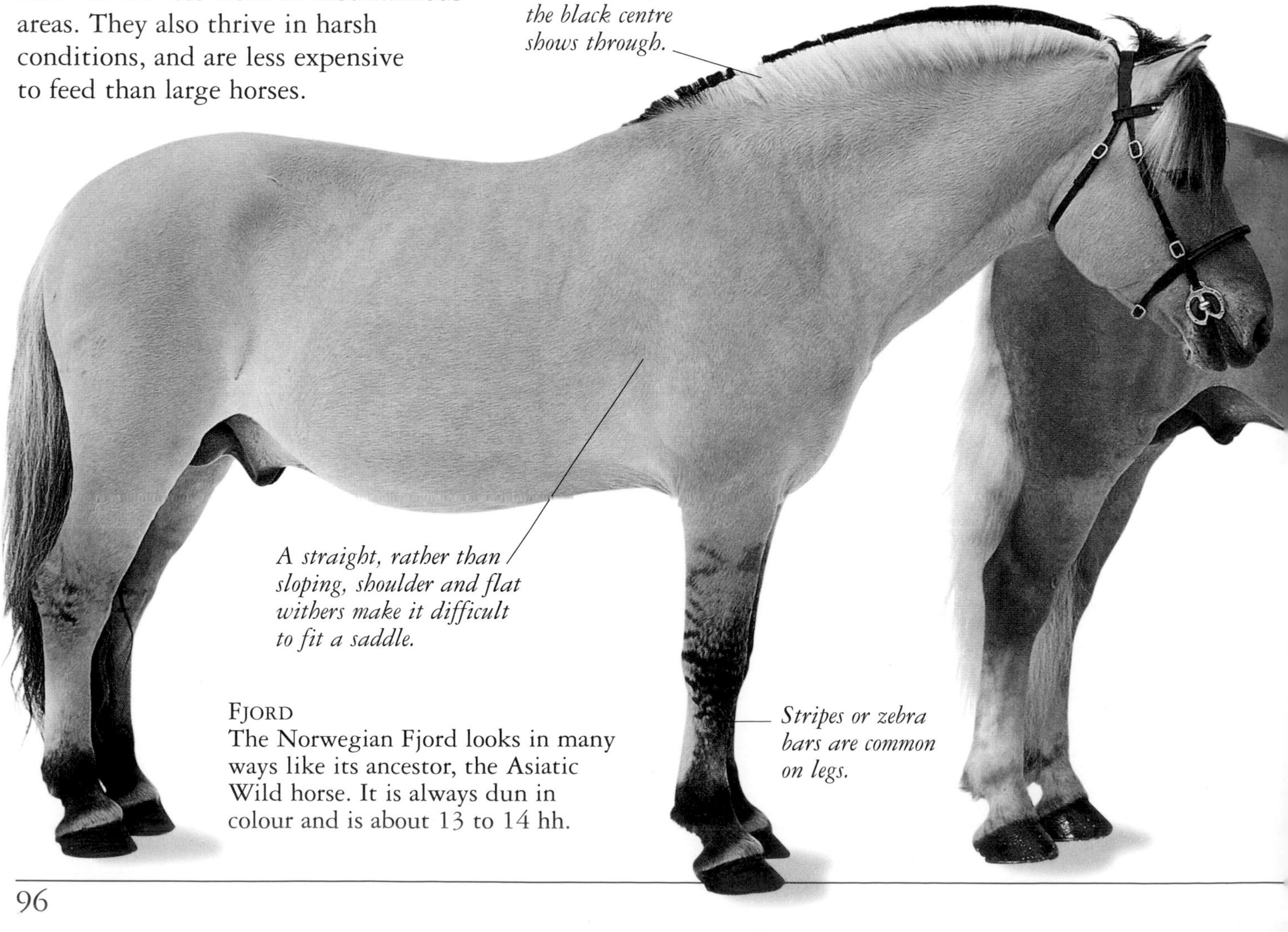

A straight, rather than sloping, shoulder and flat withers make it difficult to fit a saddle.

FJORD
The Norwegian Fjord looks in many ways like its ancestor, the Asiatic Wild horse. It is always dun in colour and is about 13 to 14 hh.

Stripes or zebra bars are common on legs.

The Piebald Pottok stands up to 13 hh.

A straight back and flat withers are common characteristics.

The shape of the legs is improved by Welsh Section B and Arab blood.

Brown, black, bay, and liver chestnut, often with white markings on the head, are the most common colours.

POTTOK
The Pottok is a semi-wild pony from the Basque region of France. There are three types: the Standard, the Piebald, and the Double.

LANDAIS
The Landais is an established French pony breed with Welsh and Arab influence. It is hardy and willing, and stands between about 11 and 13.2 hh.

Thick, flaxen mane, like tail

Open nostrils for easy breathing in oxygen-poor mountain air.

HAFLINGER
The Austrian Haflinger is always chestnut or palomino and ranges from 13.2 to 15 hh. It is the most attractive and adaptable of the European breeds.

SNOW PONIES
Sleighs pulled by Haflingers are a special attraction in the Austrian mountains. Ponies are not put in a harness until they are four years old, and many work until they are about 30.

PONIES WORLDWIDE

ALL PONIES AND horses are bred to carry out specific tasks. As the type of work ponies are bred for changes, so do the qualities and characteristics that breeders aim for. This has led to the creation of new breeds, such as the Pony of the Americas, and miniature breeds, such as the Falabella. Some breeds for example the Caspian are kept for riding, others such as the American Shetland are used for driving, and some like the Bashkir even provide milk.

Pony of the Americas
The Pony of the Americas was first bred in 1954 and is a cross between a Shetland and an Appaloosa. It is now a recognized breed, prized for its spotted coat and its suitability as a riding pony.

The pony's height is set between 11.2 and 13.2 hh.

Small and beautiful
Falabellas and miniature Shetlands are bred to be as small as possible. They are too small to be ridden, and some people believe that this is wrong. There is certainly a danger that breeding to create a small animal increases the risk of weakness, such as loss of strength and a poor constitution.

Back is straight and tail carried high.

Perfectly proportioned head

FALABELLA
The Falabella takes its name from an Argentinian family that developed the breed. It is really a horse but is never more than 76 cm (30 in) tall and it is generally called a pony.

Luxurious tail growth, like mane

Fine coat offers little protection against harsh weather.

CASPIAN
The Caspian is probably a forerunner of the Arabian horse. It is an elegant riding pony, suitable for small children, and it stands between 10 and 12 hh.

Short back and strong hindquarters

Curly coat can be clipped and spun into coarse cloth.

Long legs can be a weakness, but the Timor is sure-footed.

Flared nostrils and short ears are characteristic of this breed.

Hard hooves do not need to be shod.

Bashkir

The Bashkir is a Russian breed famed for its curly coat. It is a stocky pony of about 14 hh which can withstand sub-zero temperatures.

Timor

Named after the Indonesian island where it originated, the Timor stands between 9 and 11 hh. It is usually bay, black, or brown and is sure-footed and agile.

Well-shaped withers

Long neck

Tail, and mane, hair is fine and silky.

AMERICAN SHETLAND
The American Shetland is very different from the native Shetland pony and has Hackney, Arab, and Thoroughbred blood. It stands about 10.2 hh and is bred to drive.

Trained with weighted shoes to encourage a high-stepping action like that of the Hackney.

WARMBLOODS

THE TERM WARMBLOOD describes horses that are a mixture of either Thoroughbred or Arab, and other breeds. It is also used for European sports horses that have Thoroughbred influence but have been carefully bred. Warmbloods are tested for athleticism, soundness, and good conformation. They now dominate international dressage and showjumping.

WARMBLOODS

- Thoroughbred or Arab crosses with heavier horse breeds
- Modern sports horses bred for specific needs
- Powerful and flexible movement
- Bred from specialized dressage or jumping bloodlines
- Trainable, courageous, with kind temperaments

Hanoverian

The Hanoverian is the best-known warmblood. Its ancestry can be traced back to 1735 at Celle in Germany. This breed was originally heavier than those today, which have a greater percentage of Thoroughbred blood to give them power and elegance.

Neck is well set and long.

Noble, attractive head

Powerful hindquarters for jumping

Strong back helps the horse perform advanced dressage movements.

Wide, open-angled throat helps the horse to flex and work on the bit when performing.

Dressage demands concentrated and repetitive training.

ATHLETIC AND FLEXIBLE
Good movement is the secret of the Hanoverian's success and popularity. Its strong back and hindquarters give it the power required for dressage and jumping.

Better-shaped hooves than original examples of the breed.

DRESSAGE
The Hanoverian's good conformation, controlled movement, and courageous temperament fulfils the demands of top-level dressage.

Back length is in perfect proportion.

Withers and neck angles are ideal for a riding horse.

Thoroughbred blood has improved back conformation.

Powerful shoulders for jumping

Good hooves and forelegs

Danish warmblood

Denmark's sport horse has been developed over the past 30 years by crossing the Frederiksborg, a Danish carriage horse, with Thoroughbred and Thoroughbred crosses. The Danish warmblood is more elegant than the Hanoverian and is renowned for its kind nature.

Dutch warmblood

The Dutch warmblood is a combination of the Gelderlander, a carriage horse breed, the heavy Groningen, and the Thoroughbred. It excels in both showjumping and dressage. Mated with Thoroughbred mares, it produces elegant but powerful offspring.

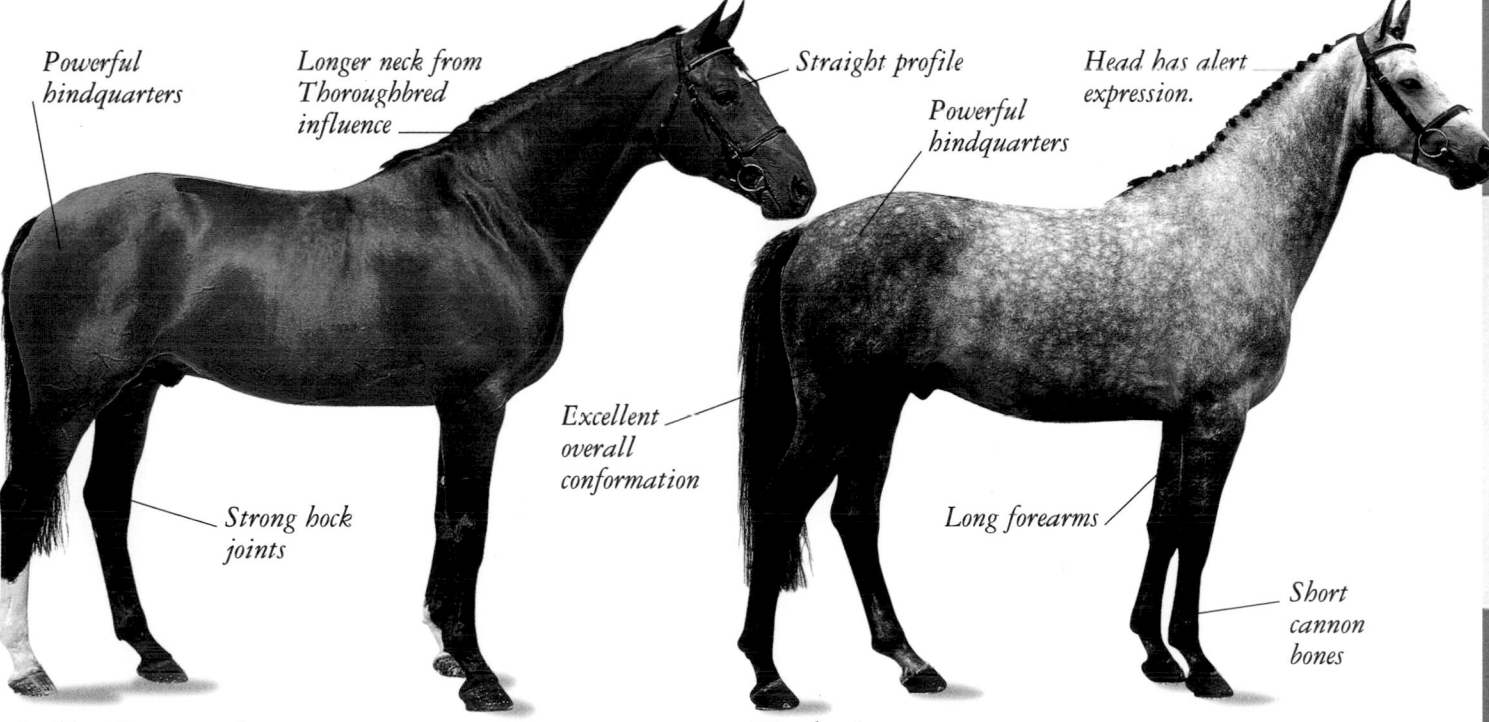

Powerful hindquarters

Longer neck from Thoroughbred influence

Straight profile

Head has alert expression.

Powerful hindquarters

Excellent overall conformation

Strong hock joints

Long forearms

Short cannon bones

Selle Francais

France's warmblood is unique in that its ancestry is with the trotting horse. It has been refined by Thoroughbred and Anglo-Arab blood. The result is a horse that excels mainly at jumping, but has the speed and agility for eventing.

Trakehner

The Trakehner originated in East Prussia, now part of Poland, and is a model of the ideal competition horse. It combines elegance with a substantial frame and its courageous and willing temperament allow it to excel in all areas.

IRISH DRAUGHT AND CLEVELAND BAY

THE IRISH DRAUGHT and Cleveland Bay were originally bred to pull carts. Today these breeds are mainly crossed with Thoroughbreds to produce competition horses. The Irish Draught is a particularly popular influence on horses bred for showjumping and eventing.

TALENT FOR JUMPING
Irish Draught blood breeds many talented showjumpers. Great strength in the hindquarters, agility, and boldness are its hallmarks.

Irish Draught

The Irish Draught is deep-bodied with good legs. Bred for agricultural work, it was also expected to carry Irish farmers out hunting. This helped to develop an athletic, sure-footed horse.

Neck length in proportion to body

Tail is black, as is the mane.

Strong hindlegs and quarters for jumping

Deep girth helps maintain stamina

Deep chest and a sloping shoulder give strength and good length of stride.

Black lower legs

Large hooves that can be too low in the heel

SPORTS HORSE
The modern Irish Draught is crossed with the English Thoroughbred to produce a sports horse conformation. It is now longer in the neck and less likely to have flat feet than the older type of Irish Draught.

Bavarian warmblood

The Cleveland Bay has had a strong influence on the Bavarian warmblood, one of the lesser-known warmblood sports horses. In the 18th century, partbred Cleveland Bay stallions were imported to Bavaria to give greater substance to the horses bred there.

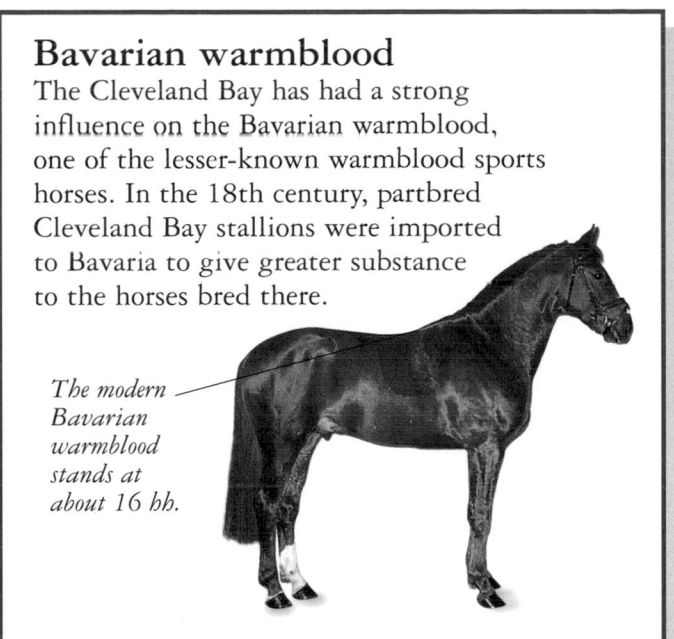

The modern Bavarian warmblood stands at about 16 hh.

CARRIAGE HORSES
The Cleveland Bay has always been a royal carriage horse in the UK, and is still kept by the royal family. Cleveland stock has been sent all over the world, particularly to the US.

Cleveland Bay

This breed is always bay with black points (mane, tail, ear tips, and lower legs). Its head is said to show influence from the Andalucian.

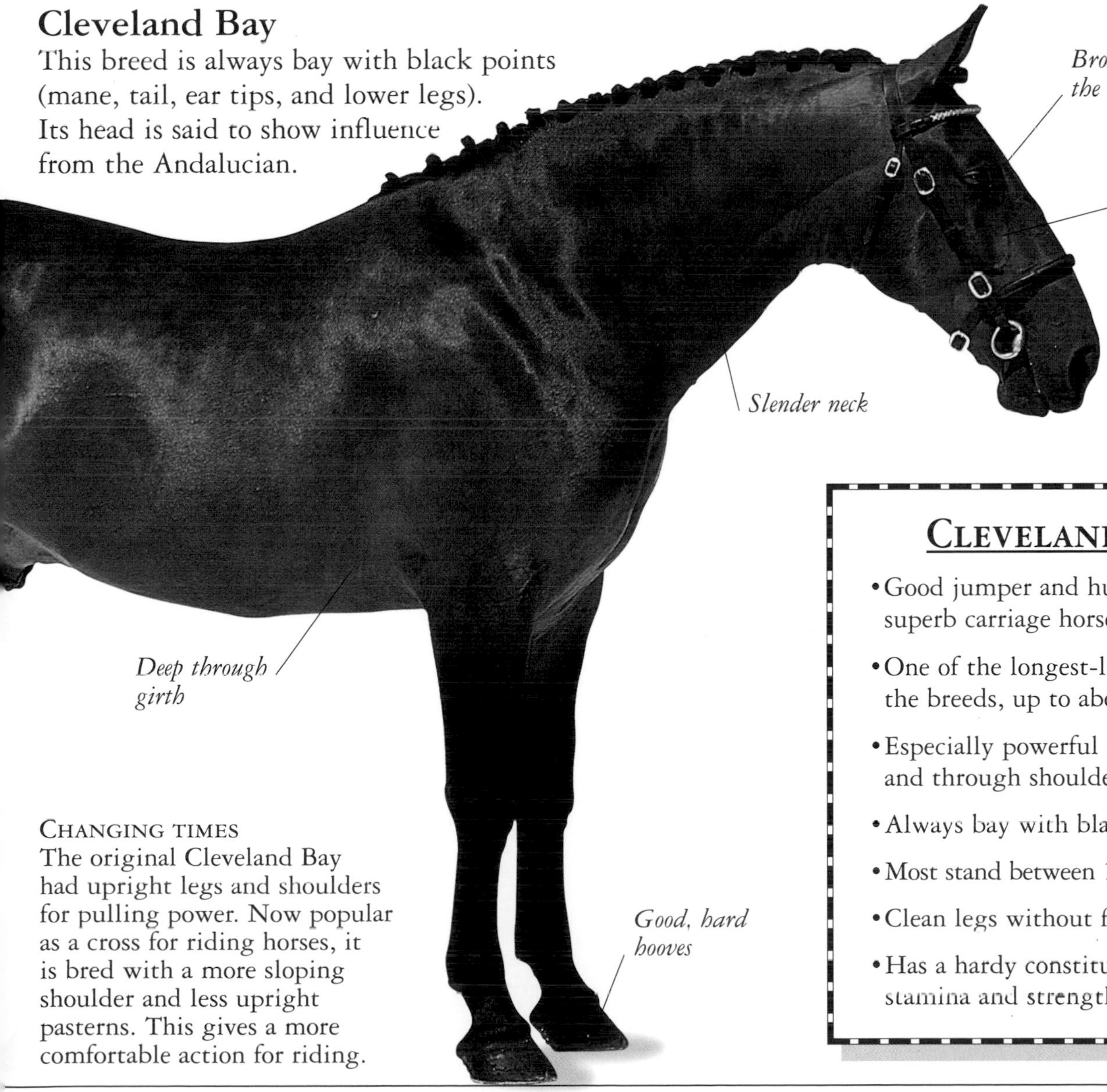

Broad between the eyes

Large head

Slender neck

Deep through girth

CHANGING TIMES
The original Cleveland Bay had upright legs and shoulders for pulling power. Now popular as a cross for riding horses, it is bred with a more sloping shoulder and less upright pasterns. This gives a more comfortable action for riding.

Good, hard hooves

CLEVELAND BAY

- Good jumper and hunter and a superb carriage horse
- One of the longest-living of all the breeds, up to about 30 years
- Especially powerful in neck and through shoulder
- Always bay with black points
- Most stand between 16 and 16.2 hh
- Clean legs without feather
- Has a hardy constitution, plus stamina and strength

HEAVY HORSES

HEAVY HORSES are the giants of the horse world. Bred to work on the land and to pull heavy loads, they are usually not less than 16.2 hh and often reach heights in excess of 17 hh. The oldest heavy horse breed is probably the Ardennais from France and Belgium, which can be traced back more than 2,000 years. The Shire is the best-known heavy horse and is descended from the medieval war horse.

Thick mane

Percherons are often dapple grey.

Percheron

The Percheron is the lightest of the heavy horses, but it is still very powerful. It has no feather and is prized for its calm and pleasant temperament.

Belgian Draught

Also known as the Brabant, the Belgian Draught has had a great influence on other breeds. Its bloodlines have contributed to the development of the Shire, the Clydesdale, the Suffolk Punch, and the Irish Draught. It is bred mainly in Belgium but is popular in the US.

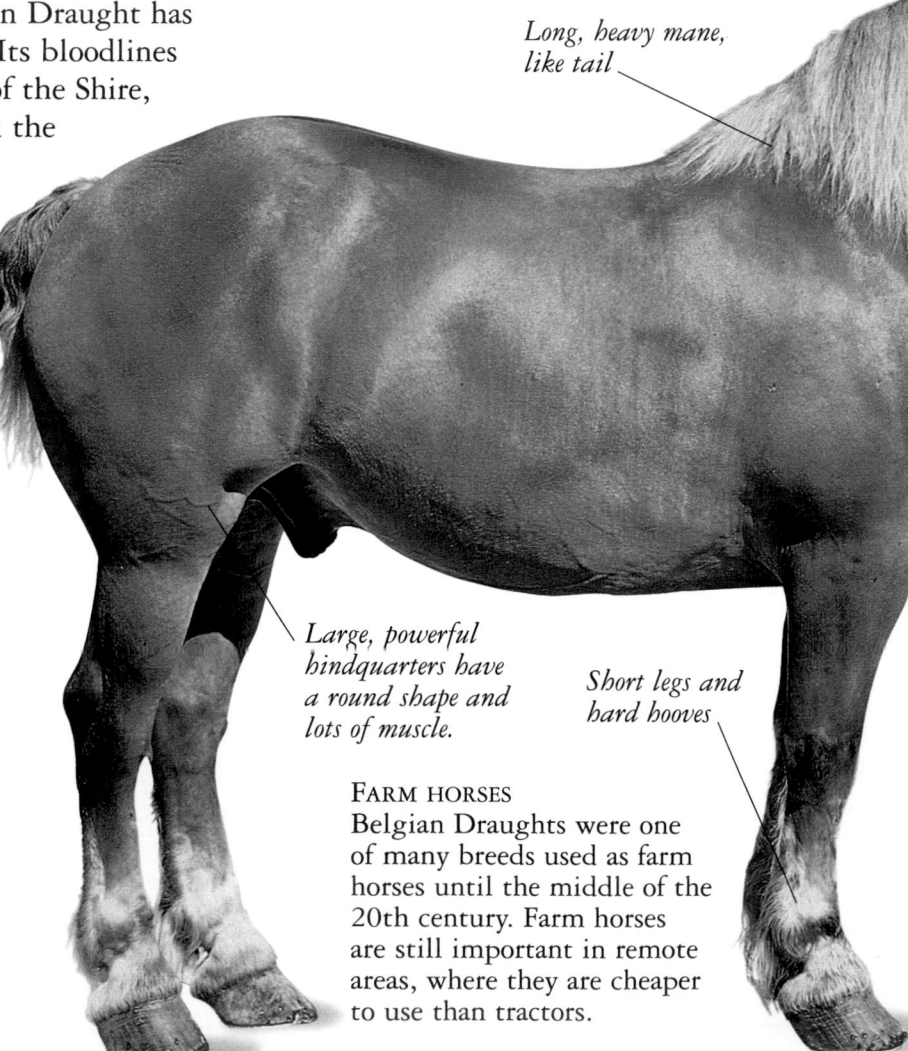

Long, heavy mane, like tail

Tail is traditionally tied up for work.

Large, powerful hindquarters have a round shape and lots of muscle.

Short legs and hard hooves

FARM HORSES
Belgian Draughts were one of many breeds used as farm horses until the middle of the 20th century. Farm horses are still important in remote areas, where they are cheaper to use than tractors.

Funeral horses

The Friesian is the lightest of the coldblooded breeds. It is mainly a harness horse and is popular for pulling hearses because of its black coat. The Friesian can be ridden and has a energetic trot.

The Friesian stands 15 hh and upwards.

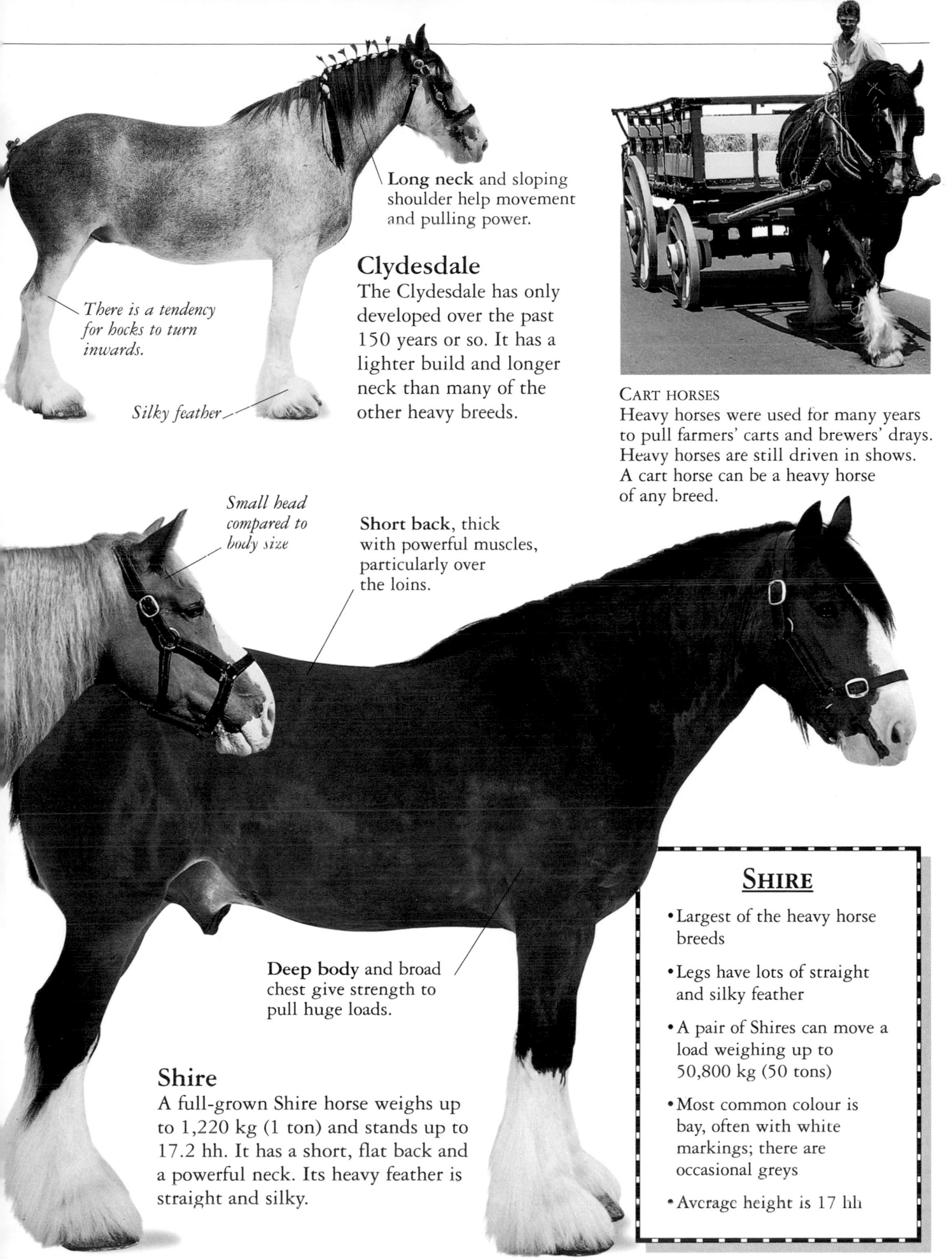

Long neck and sloping shoulder help movement and pulling power.

Clydesdale
The Clydesdale has only developed over the past 150 years or so. It has a lighter build and longer neck than many of the other heavy breeds.

There is a tendency for hocks to turn inwards.

Silky feather

CART HORSES
Heavy horses were used for many years to pull farmers' carts and brewers' drays. Heavy horses are still driven in shows. A cart horse can be a heavy horse of any breed.

Small head compared to body size

Short back, thick with powerful muscles, particularly over the loins.

Deep body and broad chest give strength to pull huge loads.

Shire
A full-grown Shire horse weighs up to 1,220 kg (1 ton) and stands up to 17.2 hh. It has a short, flat back and a powerful neck. Its heavy feather is straight and silky.

SHIRE
- Largest of the heavy horse breeds

- Legs have lots of straight and silky feather

- A pair of Shires can move a load weighing up to 50,800 kg (50 tons)

- Most common colour is bay, often with white markings; there are occasional greys

- Average height is 17 hh

PRIZED FOR COLOUR

MANY HORSES are popular because of their coat colours. They include skewbalds and piebalds, Pintos, Appaloosas, and palominos. Some, such as Appaloosas, are classed as breeds, while others, such as palominos are types. In some breeds and types the colour and pattern of the coat is always the same.

In some countries travellers prefer skewbalds to horses of solid colour.

SKEWBALDS
Skewbalds are brown and white and piebalds are black and white. They were prized by the native Americans.

Spotted horses

Appaloosas are often called spotted horses. There are also spotted ponies. The American Appaloosa was developed by the Nez Percés in the 18th century. The Pony of the Americas is a cross between the Appaloosa and the Shetland.

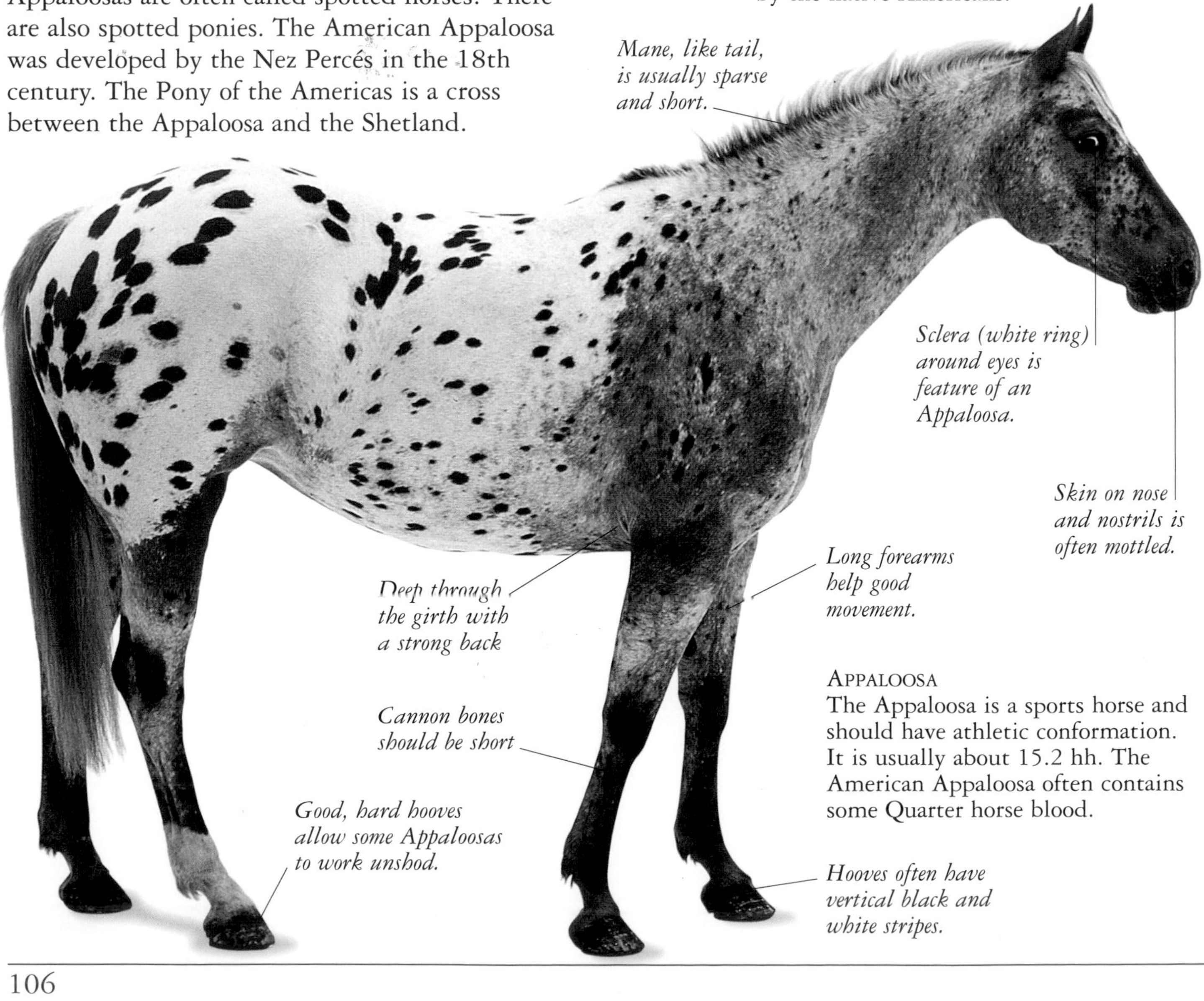

Mane, like tail, is usually sparse and short.

Sclera (white ring) around eyes is feature of an Appaloosa.

Skin on nose and nostrils is often mottled.

Deep through the girth with a strong back

Cannon bones should be short

Long forearms help good movement.

Good, hard hooves allow some Appaloosas to work unshod.

APPALOOSA
The Appaloosa is a sports horse and should have athletic conformation. It is usually about 15.2 hh. The American Appaloosa often contains some Quarter horse blood.

Hooves often have vertical black and white stripes.

Colours not breeds

In most countries, horses such as skewbalds and palominos differ widely in build, from elegant riding horses to cobs and draught animals. They are therefore classed as types, not breeds. In the US, many horses of specific colour are bred to a particular type and are classed as breeds.

Arab influence is often noticeable in tail.

White markings only appear below the knees.

A palomino's coat contains less than 15 per cent dark hairs.

PALOMINO
The perfect palomino is the colour of a newly minted gold coin, with a white mane and tail. It often has a high percentage of Thoroughbred or Arab blood.

Breed colours

Suffolk Punches and Cleveland Bays are always the same colour. The Cleveland Bay is always bay, and the Suffolk Punch is always one of seven shades of chestnut. If either breed is crossed with a Thoroughbred, the colour is often, but not always, passed on.

Traditional mane decorations

Powerful, sloping shoulder

Deep and round-bodied on powerful short legs

Round, hard hooves are smaller than many heavy breeds.

SUFFOLK PUNCH
The Suffolk Punch is a heavy horse bred to work on the land. Unlike most other heavy horses, it has very little leg hair or feather.

Pattern variations

Appaloosas and Pintos both have a number of recognized coat patterns. Appaloosas are either leopard, blanket, snowflake, marble, or frost. Leopards have white backs and hips with dark spots. White blankets are white over the hips. Snowflakes have widespread dark spots, marbles have mottled body colouring, and frosts have dark coats with white flecks. Pintos have two coat patterns – tobianos have white areas that start from the top of the body and extend down. White overos have white areas that start from the lower body.

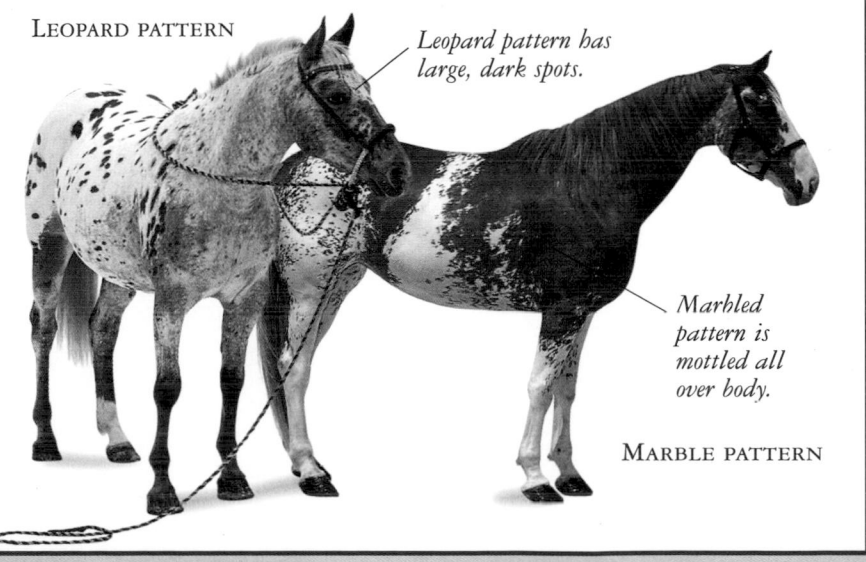

LEOPARD PATTERN

Leopard pattern has large, dark spots.

Marbled pattern is mottled all over body.

MARBLE PATTERN

GAITED HORSES

MOST HORSES and ponies have four natural gaits; walk, trot, canter, and gallop. However, some breeds have special gaits and are known as gaited horses. These gaits make the horses particularly comfortable to ride or look spectacular in harness. A gait is a natural characteristic of a particular breed, but may be encouraged and exaggerated with special training.

Traditionally shown with long, flowing manes and tails.

COMFORTABLE RIDE
Tennessee Walking horses are said to be the most comfortable of all riding horses. The breed is calm and kind, which makes it suitable for beginner and experienced riders alike.

Tennessee Walking horse

The Tennessee Walking horse originated in the southern states of the US and has Spanish ancestry. This breed looks quite ordinary when standing still, but its smooth, gliding gaits make it look very special when moving. It has three gaits; a flat or ordinary walk, a running walk, and a rocking horse canter.

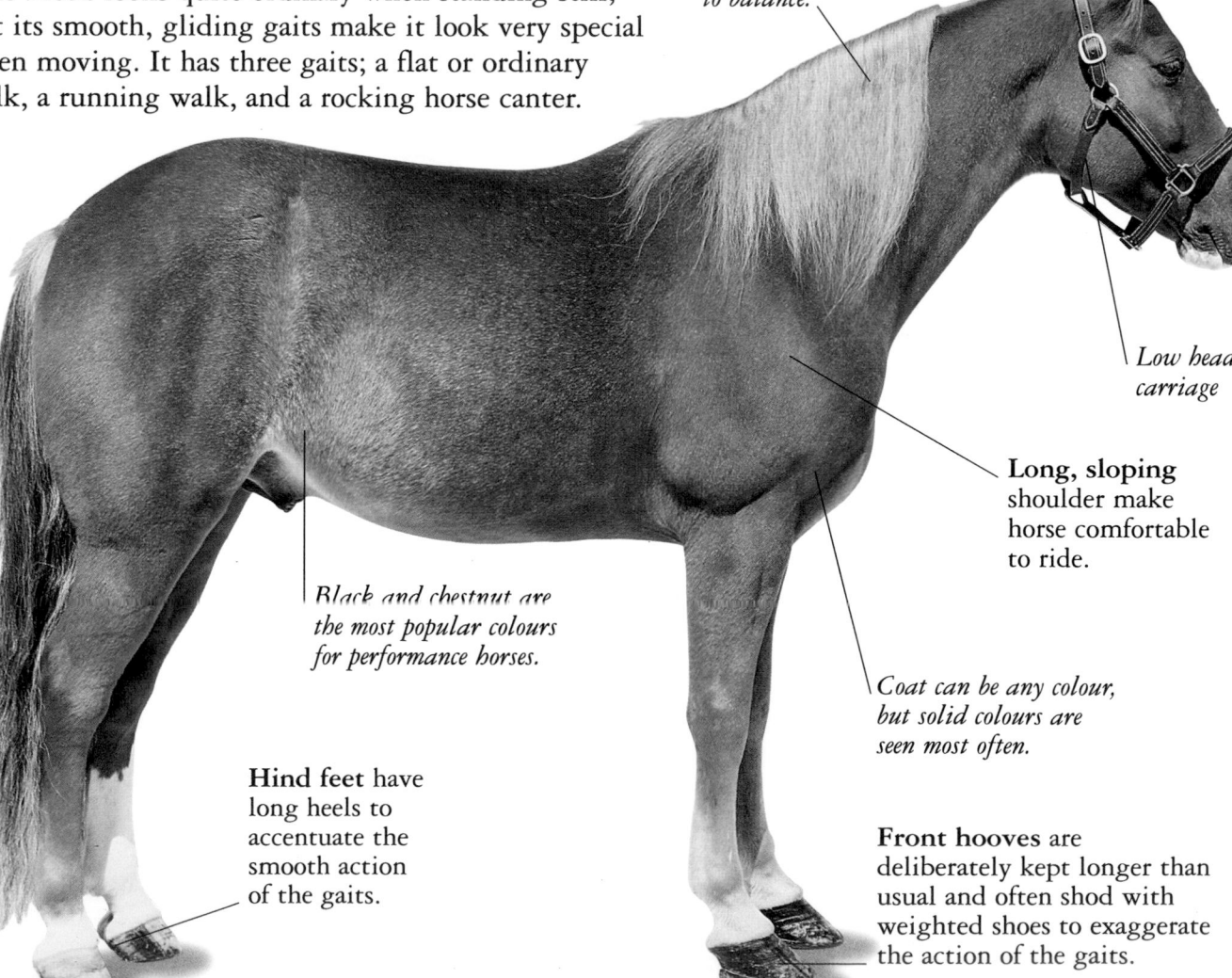

Long, elegant neck helps horse to balance.

Low head carriage

Long, sloping shoulder make horse comfortable to ride.

Black and chestnut are the most popular colours for performance horses.

Coat can be any colour, but solid colours are seen most often.

Hind feet have long heels to accentuate the smooth action of the gaits.

Front hooves are deliberately kept longer than usual and often shod with weighted shoes to exaggerate the action of the gaits.

Tail is set far up on the quarters and is carried high naturally.

At rest the Hackney should stand square, with its front legs straight and hindlegs back.

The Paso can trot at 26 kmph (16 mph) while still giving a smooth ride.

Hackney

The high-stepping Hackney is famous for its flamboyant trot. It is uncomfortable to ride, but makes a spectacular driving horse. There are Hackney ponies, which stand up to 14 hh, and Hackney horses, which reach about 15.3 hh.

Peruvian Paso

The Paso descends from horses brought to Peru by 16th century Spanish explorers. The Paso can canter, but is best known for its trot. Its three trots are called Paso Corto, Paso Fino, and Paso Largo; ordinary, slow, and fast.

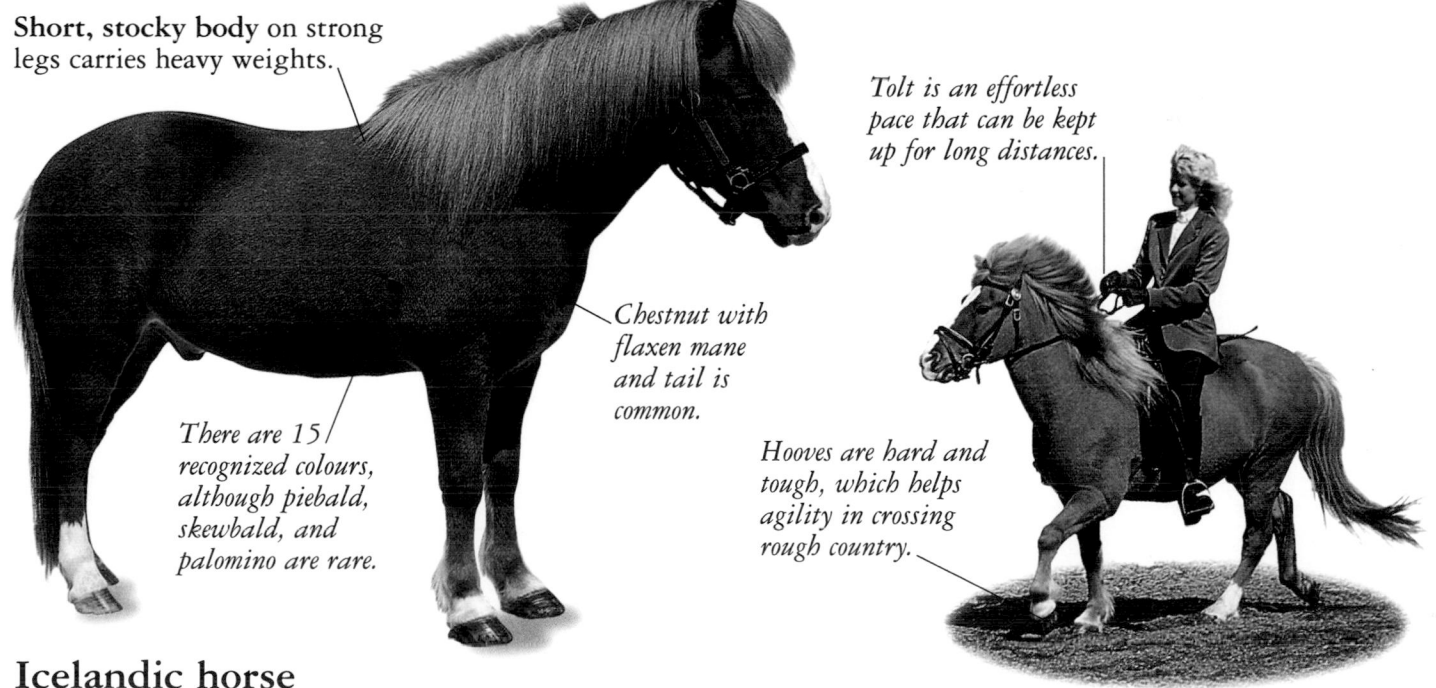

Short, stocky body on strong legs carries heavy weights.

Chestnut with flaxen mane and tail is common.

There are 15 recognized colours, although piebald, skewbald, and palomino are rare.

Tolt is an effortless pace that can be kept up for long distances.

Hooves are hard and tough, which helps agility in crossing rough country.

Icelandic horse

Although the Icelandic horse never stands more than 13.2 hh and is often smaller, it is always called a horse and never a pony. It is very strong for its size and is ridden by adults, even in races.

TOLT
The Icelandic horse has five natural gaits. The most famous is the tolt, a running walk that is used to cross uneven ground at speed.

HORSES FOR HERDSMEN

HORSES AND HERDSMEN have always been natural partners. A rider on a trained horse can herd sheep, cattle, and even other horses, while people on foot or in motor vehicles would fail. Some breeds, such as the Camargue horse and the Quarter horse, have been developed especially for herding. A good herdsman's horse is fast and agile and learns to anticipate its rider's next command.

Australian Stock horses have Thoroughbred-type heads; others, with Quarter horse blood, have squarer faces.

Rounding up sheep

Wherever sheep are kept, horses and ponies are used to move them from one place to another. The Australian Stock horse, Exmoor pony, and Welsh Cob are all perfect for this type of work.

Fine mane shows Thoroughbred and Arab influence.

Powerful shoulder and long neck help horse to keep its balance at speed and when making sharp turns.

Strong legs

Stockmen may ride with one hand.

AUSTRALIAN STOCK HORSE
The Australian Stock horse has Thoroughbred and Arab blood, and is usually between 15 and 16.2 hh. It descends from horses brought to New South Wales about 200 years ago.

Tough, hard hooves

STAMINA AND ENDURANCE
Australian sheep station workers cover long distances in high temperatures. Their horses do not have to be fast, but do need plenty of stamina and great endurance.

Work and play

The early American settlers used their cattle horses in harness and for entertainment. The favourite sports were sprint races over short distances and cattle cutting competitions.

Muscular hindquarters for turning power

CUTTING HORSES

A herd rider often has to single out one cow or calf from the rest of the herd. This activity is called cutting. Many good cutting horses are Quarter horses and they are highly prized for their abilities.

QUARTER HORSE

The Quarter horse was used for work and sport. It was traditionally raced over a quarter of a mile, which is how it got its name.

Joints must be strong to take stress of sharp turns and halts.

Herding cows

In some parts of France, the US, Australia, and other countries, horses are still used to round up cattle. Camargue horses bred in France, herd wild black bulls, which can be fierce and aggressive.

Thick tail for protection against flies

Halters, made from twisted horsehair, are worn by Camargue horses.

CAMARGUE HORSE

Although the Camargue horse only stands between 13.2 and 14.2 hh, it is always called a horse rather than a pony and is very powerful. The Camargue horses have lived wild in the Rhône delta for over a thousand years.

AMERICAN COWBOYS

Although there are few true cowboys today, some horses are still used to round up cattle. Cowboys need horses that are both intelligent and well trained.

WILD HORSES

TODAY THERE IS only one truly wild horse – Przewalski's horse. However, there are many other types and breeds, such as the Mustangs from western America and the Brumbies from Australia, that are often called wild but are in fact feral. These horses have ancestors that were domesticated but later escaped into the wild, where they formed herds. Wild and feral horses have to survive on poor quality and often scarce grazing.

Stallions will fight others if provoked.

RUNNING WILD
Horse herds consist of mares, foals, and young horses. Each herd is led by a stallion, which defends the territory, and there is also a lead mare that dominates the other mares.

Feral horses
Wild and feral horses are often resented by farmers because they graze on land needed for livestock. Mustangs are protected by law in the US and some are caught and domesticated to try and safeguard the future of the breed.

Zebras and asses
Zebras and asses belong to the same family as the horse. All are related to *Pliohippus*, the first horse ancestor to run on one toe. The African wild ass is the relative of the domesticated donkey. There are several different species of zebra including the common zebra, and Grevy's zebra.

Every zebra has a unique striped pattern.

An ass, when crossed with a horse produces a mule.

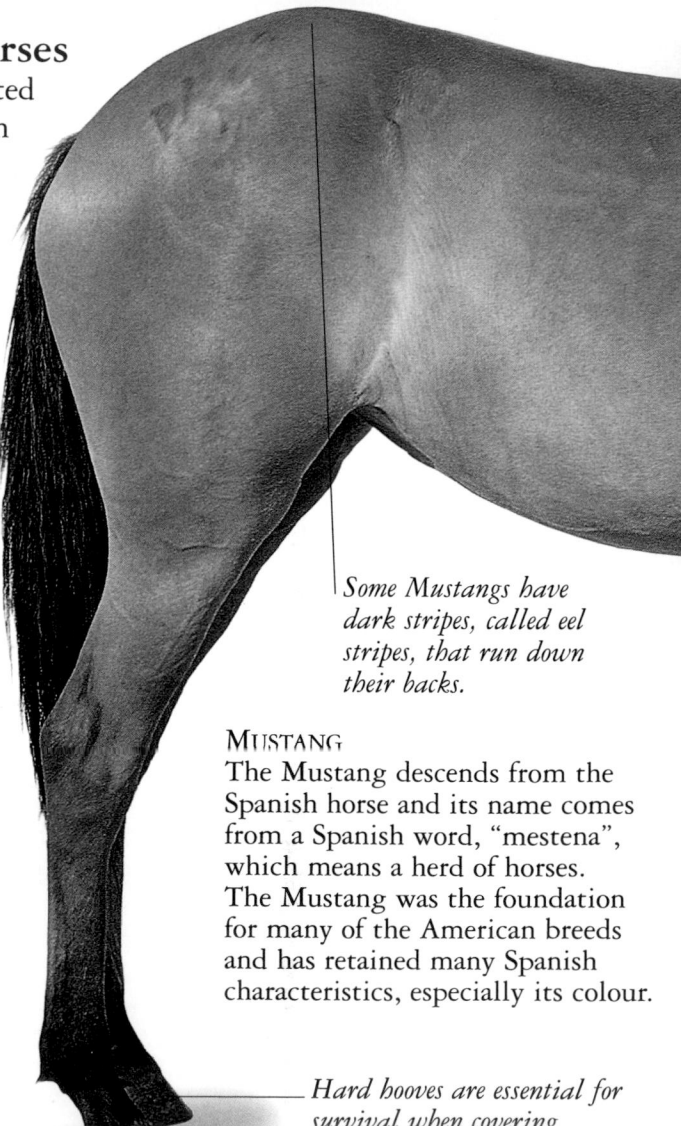
Some Mustangs have dark stripes, called eel stripes, that run down their backs.

MUSTANG
The Mustang descends from the Spanish horse and its name comes from a Spanish word, "mestena", which means a herd of horses. The Mustang was the foundation for many of the American breeds and has retained many Spanish characteristics, especially its colour.

Hard hooves are essential for survival when covering large areas of land.

Narrow body generally lacks muscle.

Sable Island ponies
Sable Island is an island off Nova Scotia, Canada. It is home to a herd of about 250 wild ponies descended from ancestors that are supposed to have swum ashore from a wrecked ship in the 17th century.

Elegant neck and head reveals Spanish ancestry.

Powerful shoulder adds speed needed for survival in the wild.

Przewalski's horse
Przewalski's horse was found roaming wild on the plains of Mongolia in the late 19th century. It has a bristly mane and a light coloured muzzle and is the only truly wild horse in the world. Today Przewalski's horses are not found in the wild, but can be seen in zoos. Scientists have plans to return a herd to the wild.

Fine coats due to Thoroughbred blood

Brumbies
Australian Brumbies are descended from domesticated horses, which were turned loose in the 19th century. Brumbies are similar in type to Australian Stock horses. Like Mustangs, they are tough and hardy but unpopular with farmers since they graze on farm land.

Brumbies exist on sparse grazing and travel miles to find water.

113

HORSE AND PONY CHART

THIS CHART GIVES you an overall view of all
the horses and ponies mentioned in this book.
Use it as a quick-reference guide to look up
the differences between each breed or type.

TYPES

COB	HUNTER	HUNTER	POLO PONY	RIDING HORSE
• Any colour, usually grey • Up to 15.3 hh • Riding and driving		• Any colour • Around 16 – 16.2 hh • Hunting	• Any colour • Around 15.1 hh • Polo matches	• Any colour • Up to 15 – 16.2 hh • All types of riding

LIGHT

ANDALUCIAN	ANGLO-ARAB	APPALOOSA	APPALOOSA	ARAB
• Bay, shades of grey, mulberry • Around 15.2 hh • Dressage, parade riding	• Chestnut, bay, brown • 15 – 16.3 hh • All riding sports	• Black, brown, chestnut and white • 14.2 – 15.2 hh • Western riding, all sports		• Any solid colour • 14.2 – 15 hh • Endurance, racing
AUSTRALIAN STOCK • Any solid colour • 15 – 16.2 hh • Herding sheep and cattle, general riding	BAVARIAN WARMBLOOD • Any solid colour • Around 16 hh • All sports	CLEVELAND BAY • Bay • 16 – 16.2 hh • Riding, driving		DANISH WARMBLOOD • Any solid colour • 16.1 – 16.2 hh • Dressage, showjumping
DUTCH WARMBLOOD • Any colour, bay and brown most common • 15.2 – 16.2 hh • Showjumping, dressage	HACKNEY • Dark brown, black, bay, chestnut • 15 – 15.3 hh • Driving	HANOVERIAN • Any solid colour • 15.3 – 16.2 hh • Dressage, showjumping	ICELANDIC HORSE • Chestnut, dun, bay, grey, black • 12.3 – 13.2 hh • Riding, all sports	IRISH DRAUGHT • Any solid colour • 15.2 – 17 hh • Showjumping, all riding, hunting
LIPIZZANER • Grey • 15.1 – 16.2 hh • Dressage, driving	LUSITANO • Any colour, mainly grey • 15 – 16 hh • Dressage	PERUVIAN PASO • Any colour, mainly bay and chestnut • 14 – 15 hh • Riding	QUARTER HORSE • Any solid colour, mainly chestnut • 14.3 – 16 hh • Riding, racing, herding, cutting	SELLE FRANÇAIS • Any colour, mainly chestnut • 15.2 – 16.2 hh • Dressage, eventing, showjumping
SHAGYA ARAB • Any solid colour, mainly grey • Around 15 hh • Riding	STANDARDBRED • Any solid colour • Around 15.2 hh • Harness racing, endurance	TENNESSEE WALKING • Black and solid colours • 15 – 16 hh • Riding	THOROUGHBRED • Any solid colour • 15 – 16.2 hh • Racing, eventing	TRAKEHNER • Any solid colour • 16 – 16.2 hh • Dressage, showjumping

WILD AND FERAL

BRUMBIES	CAMARGUE	MUSTANG		PRZEWALSKI'S HORSE
• All colours • 15 – 16.2 hh • Australia	• Grey • 13.1 – 14.1 hh • France	• All colours • 13.2 – 15 hh • United States	 MUSTANG	• Dun • Around 14.3 hh • Mongolia

HEAVY

BELGIAN DRAUGHT • Bay, dun, grey, red-roan • 16.2 – 17 hh • Farm work	**CLYDESDALE** • Bay, brown, grey, black, roan • 16.2 – 17 hh • Farm work	CLYDESDALE 	**FRIESIAN** • Black • Around 15 hh • Driving, riding
PERCHERON • Dapple-grey, black • 16 – 17 hh • Farm work	**SHIRE** • Black, bay, brown, grey • 16.2 – 17.2 hh • Farm work		**SUFFOLK PUNCH** • Shades of chestnut • 16 – 16.3 hh • Farm work

PONIES

AMERCAN SHETLAND • Brown, black, bay, chestnut, roan cream, dun, grey • 103 cm (42 in) • Driving	**BARDIGIANO** • Bay, brown • Up to 13.3 hh • Riding, farm work	**BASHKIR** • Red chestnut, bay, light brown • Around 14 hh • Riding, driving, kept for milk	**CASPIAN** • Bay, grey, chestnut, black, cream • 10 – 12 hh • Child's riding	**CONNEMARA** • Usually grey • 13 – 14.2 hh • Riding, driving
DARTMOOR • Bay, black, brown • Around 12.2 hh • Child's riding, driving	**DALES** • Black, bay, brown • Up to 14.2 hh • Farm work, trekking	**EXMOOR** • Bay, brown, dun • 12.2 – 12.3 hh • Riding	**FALABELLA** • Any colour • 76 cm (30 in) • Pet only FALABELLA 	
FELL • Black, brown, bay, grey • Up to 14 hh • Riding, driving	**FJORD** • Dun • 13 – 14 hh • Riding	**HAFLINGER** • Chestnut, palomino • Up to 13.3 hh • Driving	**HIGHLAND** • Dun, grey, brown, black, bay • Up to 14.2 hh • Riding, driving, packhorse	**LANDAIS** • Any colour • 11.3 – 13.1 hh • Riding
 FELL	NEW FOREST	**NEW FOREST** • Any colour except piebald and skewbald • 14.2 hh • Riding, driving	**PONY OF THE AMERICAS** • Black, brown, chestnut and white • 11.2 – 13.2 hh • Child's riding	**POTTOK** • Any colour • 11.1 – 14.2 hh • Riding, farm work
SHETLAND • Any colour except piebald and skewbald • 101 cm (40 in) • Child's riding, driving	**TIMOR** • Bay, black, brown • 9 – 11 hh • Riding, farm work	**WELSH SECTION A** • Any colour except piebald and skewbald • Up to 12 hh • Riding, driving		
WELSH SECTION B • Any colour except piebald and skewbald • Up to 13.2 hh • Riding, driving	**WELSH SECTION C** • Any colour except piebald and skewbald • 13.2 hh • Riding, driving, trekking	**WELSH SECTION D** • Any colour except piebald and skewbald • Over 13.2 hh • Riding, driving	POTTOK	

SHOWS
&EVENTS

WHAT TO ENTER

WHATEVER SORT OF riding you enjoy, you can also compete. There are competitions at all levels to suit everyone from the beginner to the advanced rider, and from the novice horse to the experienced one. Everyone likes to win prizes, but competing is more than that. It allows you to monitor your progress and that of your horse, and have fun at the same time.

Horse and rider in harmony

Half pass is an advanced dressage movement.

Dressage

Dressage demonstrates the horse's balance and suppleness, the rider's skill, and the communication between horse and rider. Riders perform tests made up of a series of movements, which are judged for accuracy and harmony.

Rider in forward position and in balance with horse

Fly fringes are permitted in the showjumping ring for protection against flies.

Showjumping

Show-jumpers need to be balanced and athletic. Their riders' aim is to complete a course of fences without penalties for knockdowns or refusals, often against the clock. Puissance competitions have fewer fences and test how high a horse can jump. All horses and ponies can be taught to jump, but some have more natural talent for it than others.

Endurance

This is a fast-growing sport. There are local and international competitions that range from about 32 km (20 miles) to more than 160 km (100 miles). Many riders also take part in non-competitive pleasure rides of 16–24 km (10–15 miles).

Eventing

Horse trials, or eventing, is the ultimate challenge. There are three phases – dressage, showjumping, and cross-country. Top-level three-day events include steeplechase, and roads and tracks phases. Horses must be calm and obedient for dressage, bold for cross-country, and balanced and careful for showjumping.

Showing

Showing classes are judged on a horse's or pony's conformation, movement, and ride. A good show horse or pony must be well-schooled with good manners. Different countries have different types of show class. Equitation classes focus purely on the rider – the horse is not judged.

Top hats are only worn for formal occasions.

Black jacket adds to elegance.

GETTING FIT TO COMPETE

COMPETING IS HARD WORK, so you and your horse need to be fit. A programme of gradually increasing work will develop your horse's strength, suppleness, and stamina. Check that your horse is healthy before you start and that its teeth and feet are in good shape. Ask advice on what, and how much, to feed your horse. Cycling and swimming are ways to increase your fitness.

Getting your horse fit

Getting a horse fit requires different types of work. Hacking, starting with short periods of walk, then increasing to longer, faster rides, builds a horse's stamina and overall fitness. Schooling makes it more supple and helps build up muscle, while gymnastic jumping, or gridwork, makes it more athletic.

Rider works on transitions between paces and large turns to increase horse's suppleness.

A schooled horse should work on the bit when it has warmed up, so that it is well balanced and responsive to the rider's aids.

Horse should have active paces.

WEE

1 – 2

3 – 4

5 – 6

7 – 8

Wear gloves when lungeing.

HELP FROM OTHERS

If you have little time to ride your pony, knowledgeable parents or friends may be able to help. Correct lungeing is useful for ponies who are too small for adults; make sure your pony is not lunged more than three times a week, or it will get bored. When lungeing, work on both reins and increase the amount of work from 10 to 20 minutes.

Side reins encourage pony to accept the bit.

EXERCISE ROUTINE

It is important to keep an exercise routine so you can judge the progress of your horse and spot potential problems. You must feed correctly; balance forage (grass and hay) with hard feed (mix or nuts). Increase feed gradually; give more forage than hard feed.

ROADWORK	SCHOOLING & GRIDWORK	HACKING	FEED	CHECKLIST
Walk your horse on level ground for up to 20 minutes a day, building up to 45 minutes. Avoid any hill work.	*Walk should be active and balanced.*	Feed a horse on a ratio of 75–100% forage to 0–75% hard feed, such as nuts and horse mix.	If your horse is very unfit, extend the amount of walking exercise up to about six weeks.
Introduce short periods of working, rising trot. Do not work at sitting trot. Increase rides out by up to one hour.	Start to school for 15–20 minutes, twice a week. Practise different exercises, such as large circles. Introduce canter in week four.	Hack out four to five days a week. Introduce gradual hill work. Always walk downhill, but ride at a balanced trot uphill.	If in regular work, increase ratio of hard feed to 50%. *A scoop of mix*	Increase the amount of exercise a horse has before increasing its feed, not vice versa. Continue to turn your horse out daily to help it relax.
Basic work to strengthen tendons and ligaments now complete. Horse should have reached basic level of fitness.	School at walk, trot, and canter three times a week, with short hacks if necessary.	When not schooling, take longer hacks up to one-and-a-half hours. Ride up steep hills if possible.	If necessary, increase feed in line with horse's work.	Check horse's legs daily for signs of injury or lameness. Forage should not be less than 50% of diet for ponies and most horses.
Trotting poles help to improve balance.	Introduce gridwork as part of two schooling sessions a week. Gradually build up the heights and numbers of fences.	Continue with longer hacks, including steep hills. Start fast work, but on ground that will not jar horse's hooves.	Increase feed to peak level, but continue to monitor horse's condition and reduce hard feed if horse is fit enough.	Check fit of saddle. A horse that builds up muscle through schooling will continue to change shape.

CLOTHES AND TACK

Safety helmet with chin-strap

Hacking jacket with shirt and tie

Beige jodhpurs

Full-length leather boots

CLOTHES AND TACK must be safe, comfortabl• and suitable for the horse and rider, and the type of event they are entering. It is best to get expert advice on fitting tack, and to use equipment such as helmets and body protectors that meet the latest safety standards. Using damaged equipment increases the risk of accidents.

WHAT TO WEAR
This rider is dressed smartly for general riding in competition. She could enter basic dressage, showing, and showjumping classes. Higher-level competition may require more formal clothes.

Special equipment
Different types of competitions require special equipment. Dressage, showjumping, horse trials, and Western classes all have rules about what the rider and horse should wear.

Safety helmets with coloured silks are worn for eventing and long-distance riding.

Body protector helps prevent serious injury in the event of a fall.

Flash noseband prevents horse from opening its mouth, giving rider greater control.

Brushing boots protect the horse on front and hind legs.

CROSS-COUNTRY CLOTHES
Jumping at speed means that horse and rider need protective equipment. A rider may use different or additional tack, such as a breastplate for control.

Over-reach boots

SADDLES

GENERAL-PURPOSE SADDLE
The general-purpose saddle is used for hacking (trail riding), flatwork, schooling, and jumping at basic levels. Advanced riders use special saddles for particular riding disciplines, but the general-purpose saddle is used by those who enjoy all types of riding.

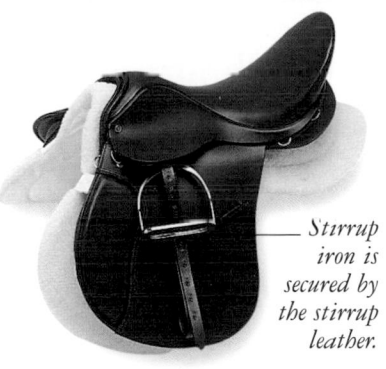

Stirrup iron is secured by the stirrup leather.

GENERAL-PURPOSE SADDLE

DRESSAGE SADDLE
This saddle is designed to make riding easier for the dressage rider, who rides with a longer, straighter leg. The saddle has straighter flaps and long girth straps, so that a short dressage girth can be used. Since there is less bulk under the dressage saddle, the horse is more responsive to the rider's leg aids.

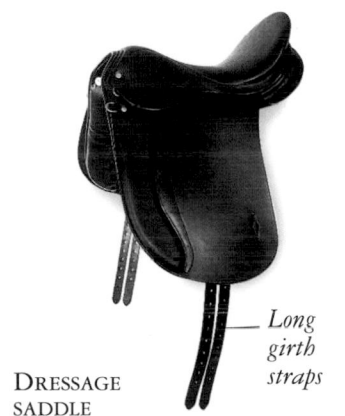

DRESSAGE SADDLE

Long girth straps

JUMPING SADDLE
The forward cut flaps of the jumping saddle make it easier for riders to ride with shorter stirrups. This helps to maintain a good forward, jumping position. Many riders use a general-purpose saddle for jumping courses up to 1 m (3 ft 3 in) but a jumping saddle is essential for bigger jumps.

Forward cut design helps rider stay in balance.

JUMPING SADDLE

BRIDLES

SNAFFLE BRIDLE
This is the simplest bridle with one bit and one pair of reins. Novice riders should use this, and it should also be used when riding young horses. There are many designs of snaffle bits and nosebands.

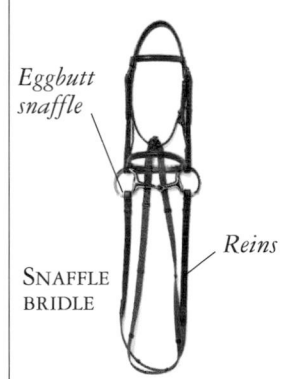

Eggbutt snaffle

Reins

SNAFFLE BRIDLE

DOUBLE BRIDLE
The double bridle has two bits and two pairs of reins that enable a dressage or showing rider to give almost invisible aids or instructions. This bridle should only be used by expert riders on well-schooled horses. It is always used with a cavesson (plain) noseband.

DOUBLE BRIDLE

Curb chain

Curb rein

Bridoon rein

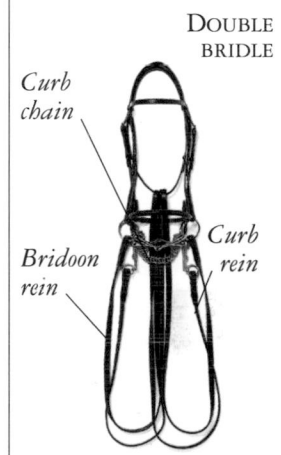

BOOTS

BRUSHING BOOTS
Brushing boots protect a horse's leg from knocks, usually from another leg. Young, unbalanced horses and those that have poor movement should always wear boots. The boots can be used on the front and back legs.

Straps must fasten on the outside of the leg.

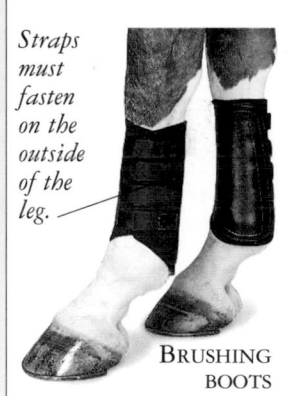

BRUSHING BOOTS

TENDON BOOTS
These boots protect the tendons on the front leg when struck by the horse's back legs. The boots are usually worn for galloping and jumping. Tendon injuries can weaken a horse for the rest of its life.

Boots fasten with clips, buckles, or velcro.

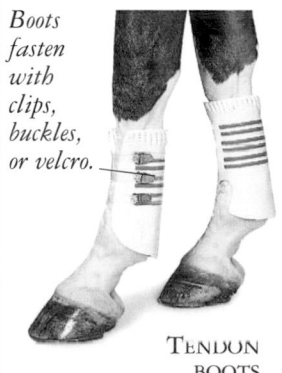

TENDON BOOTS

FOOT PROTECTORS

OVER-REACH BOOTS
These boots are fitted round the lower part of the front legs (the pastern). They protect the horse from injury when it strikes the front heel with the toe of its hind foot. Horses may do this when galloping and jumping, or if they are unbalanced.

Over-reach boots fasten around the pastern.

PETAL OVER-REACH BOOTS

GROOMED TO PERFECTION

SPECIAL GROOMING and plaiting techniques make a horse look its best for competitions. A clean, shiny coat is essential, and plaiting and quarter marks show off good conformation. Some breeds, such as Arabs and mountain and moorland ponies, should not be shown with plaited manes or tails.

QUARTER MARKS
Quarter marks show off the hindquarters. To make them, dampen the hair and make squares or diamonds by combing down against the lay of the hair. Alternatively, use a plastic template.

Quarter marks

Plaiting the tail

Many people prefer plaited tails to pulled ones, which have long side hairs pulled out. You can only plait a full tail. Take in just a few hairs at a time and keep your plait tight as you work down the tail.

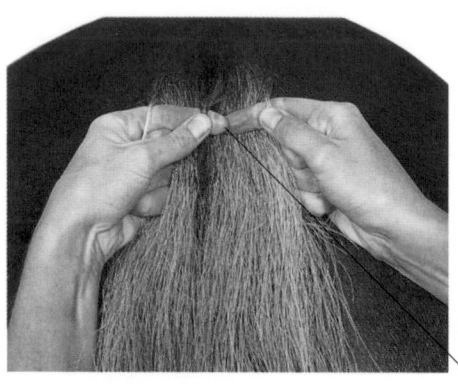

Start right at the top and keep sections tight for neatness.

1 Dividing the hairs
Take small sections of hair from each side at the top of the tail. Cross the sections over and take a third from one side of the tail and bring it to the centre.

Pass side sections over the centre.

Keep hold of the centre plait ends so that the whole plait remains tight.

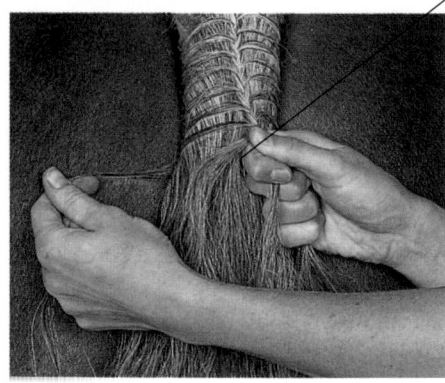

2 Plait down the tail
Bring in small sections from each side and join them with the central plait. Plait down until the centre plait reaches two thirds of the way down the dock.

3 Loop plait under tail
Continue plaiting without joining new hair. Loop the end under and stitch in place.

White socks and markings should be spotless.

Plaiting the mane

A plaited mane shows off a horse's neck. Pull or shorten the mane to about 5 in (12 cms) long before plaiting, and thin it if necessary. Although rubber bands are quick to use, plaits sewn with thread look smarter and stay in place longer.

1 Divide mane into bunches
First dampen mane with water or hair gel. Then divide the mane into as many equal bunches as suits the length of the horse's neck. Fasten each bunch with a rubber band.

2 Plait down mane
Plait each bunch, keeping the plait tight so that short hairs stay in place. Double up the end hairs and fasten with a band or plaiting thread that is the same colour as the horse's mane.

3 Roll up plait on crest
If using thread, pass needle through top of plait. Roll plait up to the crest. Stitch the plaits in place, or fasten them with rubber bands.

Some people use petroleum jelly for shine around eyes and mouth.

Whiskers may be trimmed for neatness.

Set plaits on top of a thin neck and to the side of a heavy one.

A WELL-GROOMED HORSE
Daily grooming helps to maintain healthy skin and a shiny coat. Grease and dust dull the hair. If the weather is warm, you may want to bath your horse before a competition. A little coat gloss applied with a soft cloth adds extra shine for special occasions.

Take extra care when washing the tail of an inexperienced horse.

Fetlock hair and hair around coronet neatly trimmed.

Hoof oil or polish should be used only for shows. Ask your farrier for advice on keeping hooves healthy.

Washing the tail

To wash a tail, stand to one side of the horse. Wet the hair, then work in a horse shampoo. Massage the top of the tail with your fingers to loosen grease or dirt, then work down the length of the tail. Rinse thoroughly and repeat if necessary. Squeeze out the water, then dry the tail by gently swishing it in circles.

PREPARING FOR A SHOW

START SHOW PREPARATION early; make sure your horse is fit and that your tack and equipment are in good condition. Your horse must be well shod and its vaccinations, or any other documents, must be up to date. Plan ahead and check when your class starts, then work out when you need to arrive at the show.

Pre-show preparation

Prepare as much as possible the day before a show. Clean your tack, make sure your clothes are clean, and, if necessary, bath your horse. You may want to plait your horse the day before if you have a very early start. Make a list of things you need to take and get them ready in advance.

Hard hat and gloves

Black or blue show jacket

Stock with tie pin

Long boots are usually worn by older riders. Younger riders normally wear jodhpur boots.

SHOWING CLOTHES

For a showing class or dressage wear a hard hat and gloves, and either a black or blue jacket with stock and stockpin, or a tweed jacket with shirt and tie. Choose beige breeches and long black boots or short jodhpur boots.

Travel boots for horse

Bridle

Breastplate stops saddle from slipping

Long-sleeved shirt for cross-country events

Overgirth worn over saddle in cross-country events

Saddle with girth, stirrups, and leathers

Filled haynet

Water container

First-aid kit for horse

Water bucket

Tail guard to protect tail while travelling

Mobile phone in case of emergency

Studs for shoes

Over-reach boots

First-aid kit for rider

Brushing boots

Grooming kit

Cooler rug

Feed, if needed

Grease – use on horse's legs to help it slide over fences

Long riding boots

Getting to the show

Allow plenty of time to load your horse and drive to the show. Make sure your horse wears protective travelling gear and a suitable rug. Check that you have packed all the things you need for the day before loading your horse.

Ramps should have non-slip surfaces and must be stable and level, to give the horse confidence as it walks up.

Look ahead and calmly lead horse up the ramp.

Leg guards protect horse's legs while travelling.

THE HORSE BOX
Vehicles must be light and inviting so the horse can see where it is going when loading. There must be enough headroom and each section inside the box must be wide enough for the size of horse.

Allow extra time for a young or inexperienced horse to settle when you arrive at the show.

Cover up your show clothes or change into them later.

Arrival

Try and arrive at the showground an hour before your class starts. Check that your horse has not sweated up or injured itself on the way to the show. Find out if classes are running on time, collect numbers and make entries if necessary. Tack up and walk round until your horse settles, then warm up without tiring it out.

Stand to one side in case your horse kicks out in excitement.

BEFORE SHOW

• Check horse is shod and its vaccinations are up to date

• Check clothes and tack are clean and in good condition

• If you have an early start, bath and plait horse day before show

• Check time of your class so that you can arrange to arrive at show on time

YOUR FIRST SHOW

YOUR FIRST SHOW is likely to be a small, local competition with classes for novice horses and riders. These classes may include clear round jumping, equitation classes, and competitions for best turned out horse and rider. Shows with dressage tests at beginner level are also suitable. Do not enter more than two classes or your horse may become tired, especially if it is inexperienced.

If your horse is inexperienced you may just want to watch for the first time.

What to expect

At a show, you will see lots of horses, people, and vehicles, and you may hear loud-speaker announcements. Classes are held in areas called rings, and areas where people warm up are called collecting rings. Show officials will give you a number to wear and they will tell you when it is your turn to compete.

THE COLLECTING RING

Go to the collecting ring before your class starts, as you may need to register your show number with an official. Check how many competitors there are before your turn, so that you allow yourself time to warm up. Look out for other riders in the collecting ring, especially near practice jumps. Be ready to enter the show ring when called.

If riding near parked horseboxes, watch out for other horses being unloaded.

Clear round jumping

Clear round jumping is a good introduction to showjumping for inexperienced horses and riders. You pay a small fee each time you attempt the course, and if you have problems, such as a refusal, you can try again. There is no jump-off, but usually each rider who jumps a clear round gets a special rosette. Think of it as a schooling round, not as a competition.

Rider looks ahead to next jump.

Clear round jumps are low, usually between 1 ft 6 in (45 cm) and 2 ft 6 in (75 cm). The jumps usually include small fillers and easy doubles.

ENJOYING YOUR SHOW

Shows should be fun for you and your horse. You may feel nervous at first, but concentrate on riding and caring for your horse correctly and you will soon feel more confident.

If something goes wrong, try not to panic. Keep calm, and remember that you will always have another chance, and that you and your horse will improve with practise.

	BEFORE THE SHOW	AT THE SHOW	IN THE RING	AFTER THE SHOW
PONY WELL-BEING	Allow plenty of time to load your horse into the horse box and to get to the show, so that both you and your horse are calm on arrival.	Do not ride your horse all day; get off and offer it water often. If your horse needs a feed, allow an hour for digestion before riding.	Stay calm if things go wrong. Do not panic or lose your temper – practising at home will help you avoid problems next time.	Check that there are no minor injuries or loose shoes. Once back at home, your horse should be calm and comfortable, and not sweating.
HORSE AND RIDER SAFETY	Check that your tack, clothes, and other equipment are clean and in good repair. Horse's shoes must be secure and in good condition.	Beware of excitable horses – do not ride within kicking distance of other horses. Do not ride on pedestrian-only walkways.	Walk calmly into and out of the ring.	Clean tack, clothes, and any other equipment. Check all tack for breakages and send off for repair if necessary.
RIDER MANNERS (ETIQUETTE)	Thank those who have helped you get ready for the show, such as friends and the horsebox driver. They will be happy to help you again.	Check in with ring official ten minutes before your turn. Ride in collecting ring for your class and do not monopolize the practice fence.	Be courteous to other riders. Observe instructions given by officials. Acknowledge and thank judges where appropriate.	Do not criticise judges' decisions. Avoid temptation to leave muck from horsebox at show-ground. Take all litter home.

GYMKHANAS

GYMKHANAS, or mounted games, are fast and fun. The word gymkhana originates from India; it means a meeting place for equestrian sports. Ponies are better at gymkhana games than horses because they are smaller and easier to turn and to vault on to. Riders have to be as quick and athletic as their ponies.

Mounted games

Balance and co-ordination are vital when taking part in mounted games. They can be played in teams or as individuals, and include bending races, in which riders have to ride in and out of a line of poles without touching any, and flag races, in which riders place flags in containers while on galloping ponies.

Tent pegging

Tent pegging is a military sport that began in India. An individual, or a team of four riders, carries a 3-m (10-ft) lance and gallops towards a row of tent pegs in the ground. The aim is to push the lance through the ring on the peg and lift it out without slowing down.

Fellow rider holds the pony with its reins in place, ready for the rider to vault on.

Speed and schooling

A good gymkhana pony has to be as well-schooled as a top polo pony. It must learn to twist and turn as the rider's bodyweight shifts, and to turn at speed. It is important that you do not pull on the pony's mouth, so try to teach the pony to neck rein, so that it turns from the pressure of the reins against its neck, not pressure on its mouth.

Agility and obedience is important for mounted games. The pony needs to turn tightly round cones, while the rider needs to be equally agile to stay in balance and save time.

The flag race is the gymkhana version of tent pegging.

Long sleeves protect rider's arms from scrapes in case of fall.

Vaulting

Mounting a moving pony is an essential skill for gymkhanas. To vault on, run alongside the pony for a couple of strides and use the momentum of its movement to help push you off the ground as you jump. Swing your right leg well clear of the pony's hindquarters and land in the saddle as lightly as possible.

To vault, practise running alongside your pony with the stirrups flapping. Keep feet clear of irons until mounted.

This pony wears protective tendon and over-reach boots.

131

SHOWING

WHATEVER TYPE OF horse or pony you ride, you can enjoy showing. There are classes for different breeds, types, and even colours. Some classes are judged on the horse's conformation, movement, and performance in the ring; others assess the rider's ability. There are also in-hand classes, in which the horse is led rather than ridden. Horses must always be beautifully turned out.

Ridden classes

Show horses must be schooled and well-behaved. In some classes you will be asked to give an individual show in front of the judge. This means riding your horse to show that it is obedient in all its paces. Sometimes the judge will ride each horse before deciding on final placings. You may be asked to trot your horse in-hand to show off its movement.

Showing side-saddle

Side-saddle classes are judged on either the rider's ability or the horse's conformation and suitability to be ridden side-saddle. The rider's outfit is called a habit, which consists of a jacket and an apron worn over breeches and boots.

Rider must sit straight and look ahead, not tilt to one side.

The judge may ask you to ride particular exercises, such as a figure of eight.

Standing in a line-up takes practice. Your horse must be able to stand quietly and to walk away from others when asked.

Riders should wear a black, blue, or tweed jacket.

In-hand showing

There are classes for all types of horses and ponies, including young ones, and for different types and breeds. The judge assesses a horse's conformation, so you and your horse must be able to stand still, as well as walk and trot willingly without pulling or hanging back. Your horse must also be well-behaved with others.

The handler should look smart and be able to control a horse. A hat, jacket, shirt and tie, and beige trousers should be worn.

Walk and trot your horse straight towards the judge to show how it moves.

The judge will ask riders to perform some exercises.

Riding without stirrups shows the rider's balance.

Equitation classes

If you cannot find a suitable showing class for your horse, you can have fun in equitation classes. These are judged on the rider's ability, not on the horse's looks. You will be asked to ride different exercises, such as figures of eight and riding without stirrups. Competitors may be asked to ride each other's ponies as well as their own.

> ## SHOWING
>
> • The pony and its tack must be spotlessly clean
>
> • Find out if your horse should be shown with a plaited mane. Some breeds, such as mountain and moorland ponies, are not plaited
>
> • Measure your horse, as some classes specify maximum heights for horses and ponies
>
> • Good manners and schooling are as important as good conformation

DRESSAGE

THERE ARE DRESSAGE TESTS for horses and riders at all stages of training. Tests comprise a series of movements designed to show that the horse is obedient and that the rider uses the correct aids. Beginner level tests include simple movements, such as circles.

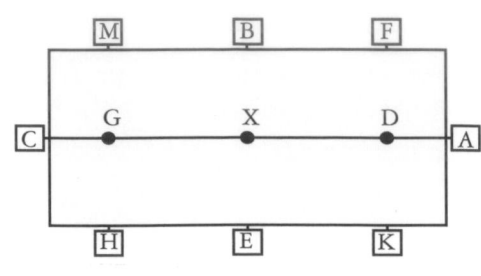

DRESSAGE ARENA
Tests for beginners are ridden in an arena measuring 40 x 20 m (130 x 66 ft). Letters around the arena indicate where a rider should start different dressage movements.

DRESSAGE MOVEMENTS	
20-METRE CIRCLE Dressage tests for beginners include the 20-metre circle, which is ridden in trot or canter. The circle can start from A, C, B, or E. Marks are deducted if the circles are squashed or egg-shaped, so ride in a true circle.	20-METRE CIRCLE
DOWN CENTRE LINE Tests always start and finish by riding down the centre line. Be positive as you ride down the line and look where you are going, so that you are able to guide your horse in a straight line.	DOWN CENTRE LINE
SERPENTINE LOOPS A three-loop serpentine is one of the most difficult movements in beginner tests. The loops must be equal in size and the rider should ride straight across the centre line before starting another loop.	SERPENTINE LOOPS
SHALLOW LOOPS Loops of 3 m (10 ft) or 5 m (16 ft) are ridden down the long side of the arena, between the two outside markers, H and K, or F and M. While riding the loop, horse and rider should maintain a steady rhythm.	5M SHALLOW LOOPS

Turnout

A dressage rider and horse should be clean, tidy, and neat. At beginner level, riders wear either a tweed jacket with a shirt and tie, or a black jacket and stock. Jodhpurs can be beige or white, and boots can be long or short.

Tails can be pulled or plaited. Pulled tails need bandaging to keep them in shape.

Rider creates energy using leg aids, but controls the pace using weight and hands, without pulling back.

Collected paces

At advanced levels of dressage, horse and rider are asked to work in collected paces. When a horse is collected, it is similar to a coiled spring, full of controlled energy. The horse's steps are shorter and higher than in other paces and its hindlegs come farther under its body. The rider sits tall and light in the saddle to present an elegant picture.

A plaited mane looks smart and helps create a good impression.

CORRECT EQUIPMENT
Riders can carry whips and wear spurs in dressage tests but must not misuse them. Martingales are not allowed but neckstraps, breastplates, and breastgirths are. Only certain bits and nosebands are allowed.

Snaffle bridles are used at beginner level.

Rider's legs create energy to lengthen stride without increasing speed.

Dressage riders should check a dressage rule book to make sure clothes and tack comply with their level of competition. Using wrong tack will result in elimination.

Hooves are oiled for competition.

Extended paces

In extended paces, the horse's stride should be as long as possible. It is important that the horse stays balanced and does not pull or lean on the rider's hands. Beginner level tests ask for lengthened strides, which are easier to perform. This is the first step to producing the extended paces of the advanced horse.

135

DRESSAGE TESTS

A DRESSAGE TEST is a series of movements performed in front of judges to show that a horse is obedient and supple, and that a rider's position and use of aids are correct. Each movement in a dressage test carries up to ten marks. At the end of the competition, the judge gives the riders a sheet with marks and comments about their test. These help riders decide what they need to practise before their next competition.

Rider practises different movements.

LEARNING YOUR TEST
Some people learn tests by drawing diagrams of the movements in the correct order; others walk the test on foot. Practise the movements with your horse, but ride them in a different order. Do not ride the complete test too many times or your horse may start to anticipate what comes next.

Top level horses often have plaits fastened with white tape.

Dressage riders plan time to warm up, making sure the horse is not too fresh or too tired when it starts the test.

Concentrate on keeping the horse balanced and energetic before entering the arena.

Bandages used for warming up must be removed before starting the test.

Make sure you know the positions of the letters.

Practise movements that you and your horse are good at. If you attempt movements that you find difficult, your horse may become tense. Concentrate on building its energy and responsiveness.

Warming up

There will probably be a special area or school for warming up at the show. Other riders will also be using the practice area so be aware of where they are going. Start your warming up on a loose rein so your horse stretches its muscles. You may need up to half an hour to warm up. Try to stay relaxed, so that you do not make your horse tense.

Riding the test

As you enter the arena, look up and smile. Try to keep your breathing steady to help you stay calm. Make sure your horse is moving energetically so you ride a straight line down the centre without leaving the centre line. If you make a mistake, keep calm – you will have lost marks for only one movement. Remember to smile and salute the judge at the end of your test.

IN THE RING

- Keep your horse moving energetically, but do not rush

- If you perform a movement incorrectly, calmly correct your mistake, if possible, then concentrate on the next movement

- Keep your breathing rhythmic, as this will help to prevent you becoming tense

Dressage judges look for a horse and rider that make an elegant picture together. Movements must be accurate and performed at the right place.

Advanced horses, such as this, wear double bridles. Beginner level horses always wear snaffle bridles.

Rider's hands are sensitive and do not pull on the reins.

SHOWJUMPING

THERE ARE SHOWJUMPING competitions for ponies and horses at all levels, ranging from small local shows to international competitions. The aim of riding a course is always to have a clear round without knocking down any fences. A course is often ridden against the clock, and the fastest clear round wins. Top-level Puissance competitions test the horse's ability to jump great heights, often 2 m (6 ft 6 in) or more.

A body protector should be worn, even when practising.

Brushing boots protect the horse's legs when it is jumping.

Novice classes

Novice classes are for inexperienced horses or riders. Fences should be low and there should be no difficult turns or tricky distances between jumps. Clear round classes, in which the aim is to jump a clear round, are an ideal introduction to showjumping. Many shows allow you to attempt more than one round so that you gain extra experience.

Distances between jumps for showjumping courses are based on a horse's canter stride measuring 3.7 m (12 ft). Ask advice when measuring distances for a pony.

SEEING A STRIDE
Learning to ride a balanced, rhythmic canter can help you meet the take-off point for a fence correctly. This is called "seeing a stride." A good way to learn how to do this is to lay a course of poles on the ground and practise riding over them in a flowing rhythm.

Rider looks ahead to the next jump.

Gridwork

Gridwork helps you and your horse to become confident and athletic. A grid is a row of fences spaced at the correct distance for a horse's stride. This makes it easier for the horse to find the correct take-off points. The distances are shorter for ponies than for horses. Get an expert to help set up the grid, and always have someone on the ground who can alter the distances if necessary.

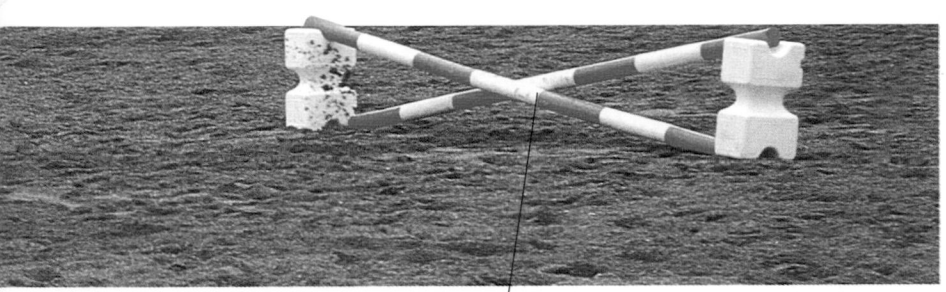

Riding a grid encourages you to improve your rhythm and to ride in a straight line.

Poles are placed at set distances on the ground.

A spread fence encourages a horse to take off correctly and jump in style.

DISTANCES BETWEEN JUMPS
Distances between fences are set to allow a certain number of strides between them. At advanced level you may need to shorten or lengthen your horse's stride to meet a fence correctly.

A double, two fences set at a distance, allows one or two non-jumping strides between a fence.

Types of jump

Fences can be uprights or spreads, and a course will have both. Courses will include rustic poles, planks, coloured fillers, brush fences, walls, and gates. Advanced courses may have water jumps. Your instructor will help you introduce your horse to different types of fence so that you and your horse approach a jump confidently.

Fillers test horse's and rider's confidence and concentration. Some horses may shy away from fillers.

IN THE RING

WHEN YOU FIRST START jumping at competitions, choose courses that have slightly smaller fences than you jump at home. This gives you and your horse confidence when jumping in strange surroundings. Walk the course carefully, and allow time to warm up before you enter the ring. If you jump a clear round and have a long wait before a jump-off, ride over two or three practice fences just before your turn.

WALKING THE COURSE
A rider can see potential challenges in the ring, such as fences on slightly uphill or downhill approaches, by walking the course. Walk the track you intend to ride so you know which route to take once you are on the horse. In novice classes, distances between combination fences are usually straightforward, but in higher level competitions distances are more complicated.

A *helper adjusts the practice fence, by gradually making it taller until it is competition height.*

Once your horse is jumping happily, stop. Do not tire a horse before it goes into the jumping ring.

Do not jump a practice fence too many times; six to ten turns is usually enough.

Warming up
Allow about half an hour to warm up before you enter the show ring. First try to make your horse obedient and attentive, then establish a rhythmic canter. Next, jump a few upright and spread practice fences. Practice fences should be no higher than the course you are competing over. Be considerate to other riders in the practice ring.

Riding the course

Enter the jumping ring calmly and set up a balanced canter until you receive the signal to start. Approach the first fence calmly but positively. Always look up and ahead to the next fence; never look back if you hit one, as this will unbalance your horse. As you change direction for each jump, make sure your horse is on the correct leg for canter; come back to trot if necessary. Finally, jump fences straight on, not at an angle.

KEY   LONG ROUTE ■   SHORT ROUTE ■

JUMP-OFF

Most jumping classes have a timed jump-off for all riders who go clear in the first round. At home, practise taking a shorter route without spoiling your horse's approach or balance. Making good turns saves more time than galloping between fences, and you will be less likely to hit poles.

Rider is looking up and ahead to next jump.

Rider is keeping light rein contact that does not restrict horse.

Rider is in perfect balance. She has folded forward from the hips, and her weight is absorbed through her knee and ankle joints.

CROSS-COUNTRY

JUMPING CROSS-COUNTRY fences requires courage from both horse and rider. Fences cannot be knocked down, and are tackled at a faster speed than showjumps. If the rider and horse wear correct protective equipment, and if the horse is well-schooled, riding cross-country can be safe and fun. Cross-country jumping can be a competition in its own right or part of a horse trial, in which riders also take part in dressage and showjumping.

Jumping technique

To be successful at riding cross-country, a rider must be able to ride at speed, while in control. The rider should maintain a rhythm with the horse's stride so that it meets fences without having to speed up and slow down each time. The rider must keep in balance with the horse even when things go wrong.

The red flag must always be on the right as you jump the fence.

Crash helmets and body protectors must be worn to minimize injury if the rider falls.

Difficult fences

Some cross-country fences are difficult and need careful riding. To tackle a water jump a horse needs power, not speed, so it does not stumble. Drop fences should be approached with energy and impulsion, but more slowly than ordinary fences. To jump a bounce fence, the rider must be balanced, so that the horse lands over one fence and immediately takes off over another without taking a stride.

JUMPING INTO DARKNESS

Jumping into darkness, perhaps from a field into woods, is difficult for a horse. The rider should approach the fence in a straight line, so that the horse can adjust its eyesight to the changing conditions. By sitting up and riding with determination, the rider can control the horse's pace.

Landing in water slows the horse down, so a controlled approach is vital.

QUICK ROUTES

On a cross-country course, there is often a choice of routes over single fences, and over combinations with more than one jump. The quicker routes are usually more difficult, and are only suitable for experienced horses and riders. If riders are unsure, they take the slower route.

Eventing

Eventing, or horse trials, is the most challenging of all equestrian sports. Riders have to perform a dressage test, then ride a cross-country course and a round of showjumps. Novice events are run over one day, and intermediate and advanced competitions take place over two and three days. Two- and three-day events include speed and endurance sections over a short course of steeplechase fences, and roads and tracks.

Breastgirth or breastplate helps prevent saddle slipping back.

Grease on horse's legs helps it slide over fences, thus preventing serious injury.

ENDURANCE RIDING

Rider and horse must be fit.

COMPETITIVE ENDURANCE rides range from 40 km (25 miles) to more than 160 km (100 miles). There are also non-competitive pleasure rides of about 16 km (10 miles). Arabs and part-bred Arabs are the most popular types of endurance horse at top-level, but any fit horse or pony should manage shorter distances.

Long-distance riding

Long-distance rides must be completed at set speeds, so riders have to judge the speed of their horses' trot and canter. Riders also monitor their horses' heart and breathing rates to make sure they pass the vet checks along the way.

Support team ensures that horse does not catch a chill.

SUPPORT TEAM
The support team, called the crew, is vital at top-level competitive endurance riding. Each rider has a crew to meet up with at various points on a long ride. The crew cools down the horse and makes sure it is comfortable; it also provides the horse with food and water when necessary.

Sloshing down is the safest way to cool down a hot horse. Members of the support team pour water over the horse and walk it round.

Endurance horses are usually allowed to eat and drink small amounts along the ride to help maintain their energy levels.

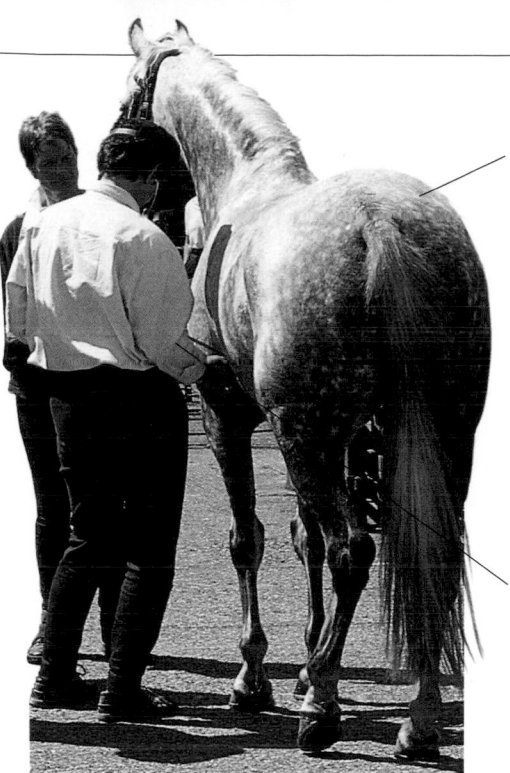

A fit horse should not get muscle cramps.

The vet will not allow a lame or sick horse to continue.

VETERINARY CHECKS
Veterinary surgeons check horses at "vet gates" – marked stages along the ride. The vets check that heart and breathing rates are correct and that the horse is not lame or injured. A horse that is breathing too fast is not allowed to continue until it has settled.

Bred for endurance

An endurance horse must have strong legs and feet, so that it can cope with long rides. The Arab has always been a popular breed with endurance riders. It has natural stamina, speed, and agility. Although lightly built, it can carry weight. Anglo-Arabs, part-bred Arabs, and Standardbreds are also popular.

An Arab has natural balance to cope with difficult terrain.

Horse trails

Organized rides lasting half a day or more are called treks or trail rides. Riders can take their own horse, if it is fit enough, or they can join an organized holiday. Horses need to be sure-footed and sensible, especially on moorland or in mountainous areas. Riders who enjoy this sort of riding may go on to take part in competitive rides.

PLEASURE RIDES
Pleasure and sponsored rides are organized rides that follow a set route; some include optional jumps. These types of rides are not competitions, but riders may be asked to raise sponsorship for a charity. Pleasure rides are a good introduction to long-distance riding for young horses, since they learn to behave in unusual surroundings.

Horses must be agile to cope with mountainous terrain.

The Kentucky Derby is run on a "dirt track". This all-weather surface does not freeze.

RACING SPORTS

MANY RACING SPORTS are for Thoroughbreds, but there are also specialist races for Quarter horses, Arabs, and harness horses. Top racehorses are among the most valuable in the world; winners of the world's most prestigious races can be worth millions. Ridden horses can be raced on the flat or over jumps. To train riding or driving horses to achieve racing speeds requires special skill and courage.

Flat racing

Some racehorses are bred to run on the flat. They are backed as yearlings and raced as two- and three-year-olds, but often retire at an early age. Flat racehorses are handicapped by weight according to their age and past performance; this makes races more competitive. Prestigious races include the Kentucky Derby, the English Derby, and the Prix de l'Arc de Triomphe in France.

Riders that race on horseback are called jockeys.

Jockeys wear crash helmets covered with coloured silks.

Steeplechasing

Thoroughbred steeplechasers start their racing careers when they are about four years old. The sport started in Ireland, when two riders raced between the steeples of two churches. Today the sport is most popular in the British Isles, but also takes place on a small scale in the US and Europe. Famous races include the Grand National in the UK and the Pardubice in the Czech Republic.

Steeplechasers jump high, fixed fences at racing speeds over distances of up to 7 km (4.5 miles).

Harness racing

Harness racers are bred to trot rather than gallop, but some reach speeds equivalent to those of galloping racehorses. Some harness racers move their legs in diagonal pairs, like riding horses, while others pace by moving their legs in lateral pairs.

Pacers race by moving lateral legs together. The left front and hind legs move at the same time, followed by the right pair of legs.

Goggles protect a jockey's eyes from flying turf and dirt.

The groom shifts her weight to help steer the carriage around the obstacles.

Contestants aim to complete the course without knocking down the balls or the cones.

Scurry driving

Scurry driving combines speed with accuracy. Drivers and ponies race around a twisting course of up to 20 pairs of bollards or cones, each pair set just wide enough apart for the wheels of the carriage to pass through. Driving trials is another popular driving sport. Similar to ridden horse trials, competitors take part in three phases: dressage, the marathon, and an obstacle course.

TEAM SPORTS

TEAM SPORTS are fast and demand special skills from horse and rider. Polo is one of the oldest and most popular of sports, while polocrosse and horseball have been introduced more recently. To take part in team sports, horses and riders must be fit. Riders need quick reactions and good balance for making fast, sharp turns. Team sports are played on ponies and small horses.

Le Trec

Le Trec began in France about 25 years ago, and is divided into three phases. The first is orienteering, in which riders follow a map at set speeds. The second judges the control of a horse's paces. The third involves jumping, cross-country, and dismounted exercises.

The net is used to scoop and throw a soft, rubber ball.

Polo

Each team has four players whose aim is to score by hitting the ball into the opposing team's goal. Player number one attacks, number four defends, while the other two mark the centre. A match consists of four to six "chukkas", each lasting seven minutes.

The attacking player must score as many goals as possible.

Riders can hook an opponent's stick.

Polocrosse

Polocrosse teams consist of six players. Each team is divided into two so that only three players from each are allowed on the pitch at a time. Player number one is the attacker and the only one who can score a goal. Player number two takes the centre position, and player number three is the defender. A match is made up of six timed sections called "chukkas", each lasting between six and eight minutes.

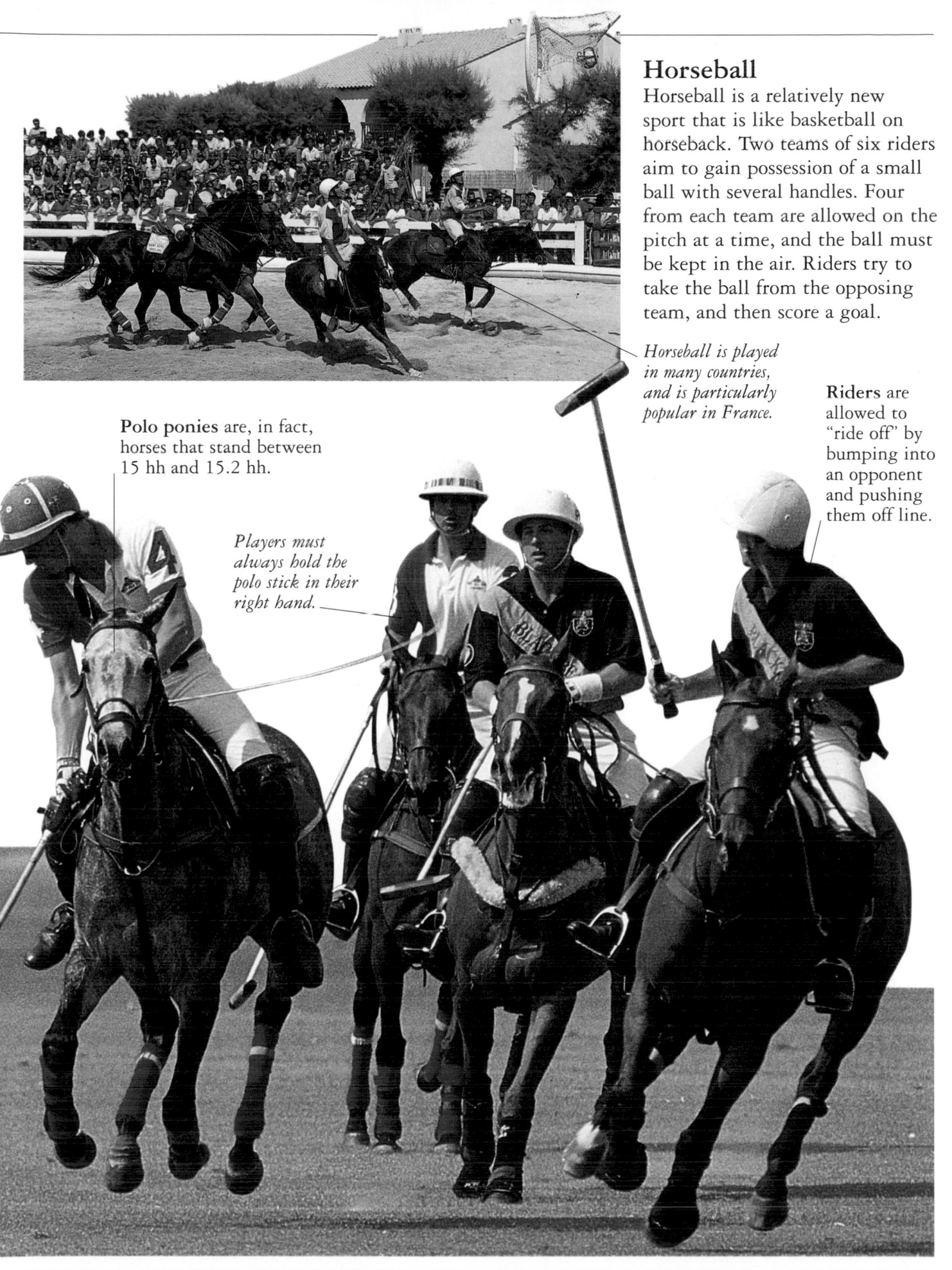

Horseball

Horseball is a relatively new sport that is like basketball on horseback. Two teams of six riders aim to gain possession of a small ball with several handles. Four from each team are allowed on the pitch at a time, and the ball must be kept in the air. Riders try to take the ball from the opposing team, and then score a goal.

Horseball is played in many countries, and is particularly popular in France.

Riders are allowed to "ride off" by bumping into an opponent and pushing them off line.

Polo ponies are, in fact, horses that stand between 15 hh and 15.2 hh.

Players must always hold the polo stick in their right hand.

HOMEWARD BOUND

WHEN YOU HAVE finished competing, tend to your horse. Before heading for home cool down your horse and check for minor injuries and loose shoes. Wash any mud from its legs to uncover hidden cuts and remove shoe studs if used. Allow your horse to drink, but make sure the water is not too cold. Once back at home, make sure your horse is comfortable before finishing for the day.

Care of grass-kept horse

At the show, cool down a grass-kept horse as you would any other horse. At home, check that the horse is comfortable; it should not be shivering and the base of its ears should feel warm. If necessary, stable and rug up the horse until it is dry and comfortable enough to turn out. Otherwise, turn it out so that it can walk around and roll.

Rolling helps dry off a sweaty coat and relaxes the horse.

Cooling down

Before going home, make sure your horse has cooled down, so that it doesn't get a chill. Walk the horse round, with a rug on if necessary; it may not need a rug in hot weather. If it is hot and humid, alternate walking your horse with washing it down until the horse is comfortable.

Muscle cramp may occur if you leave your horse standing still immediately after working hard. Walk it quietly to allow it to relax, and make sure its temperature is stable.

AT HOME

- Check for minor injuries and any heat or swelling in legs
- Make sure the horse has hay and water
- Provide horse with deep bed in its stable, so it can lie down
- If necessary, use extra rugs to keep horse warm
- Always make a final check before you finish for the day
- Check horse for lameness by trotting it first thing the next day

Unload with care. A tired horse may trip or stumble.

Coming home

Put a rug on your horse to travel home. A light rug or summer sheet is necessary even in warm weather to prevent tired muscles cramping up and as protection from draughts in a moving vehicle. Offer the horse a drink before you leave the show and give it a haynet to help it relax during the journey.

In the stable

Check that your horse has travelled well and there is no sign of injury, sweating, or heat or swelling in the legs. If you are worried, get expert advice; check the horse's legs first thing the next morning. Put on stable rugs, then make sure the horse has hay and water and a clean, deep bed. If the horse is dry and relaxed, feed as normal. Before finishing for the day, check over the horse, and add or change rugs if necessary.

Give the same quantity and type of feed as normal. Clean water must be available.

SAFETY AT A SHOW

COMPETING puts extra demands on you and your horse, so it is important to make sure you both stay safe. Use the right clothes and equipment and make sure you only take part in well-organized competitions. A veterinary surgeon and qualified first-aid experts should always be available in case of an emergency.

Special grease is smeared on the horse's legs to help it slide over cross-country fences.

Studs come in different shapes and sizes.

Brushing boots help prevent injury if the horse knocks its legs together while jumping.

Over-reach boots protect the horse's heels.

Cross-country overgirth fastens over saddle.

Rider safety

Always ride with a hat or helmet that meets the highest safety standards. It must fit properly and the harness must always be fastened. If you are jumping, especially cross-country, wear a body protector; this helps prevent injury if you fall. Replace damaged safety equipment and do not buy these items secondhand.

Horse safety

You need to protect your horse when galloping or jumping. Boots are especially important and help prevent leg injuries. They must be the right size and fastened so that they do not slip, but are not too tight. Studs that screw into the shoes give better grip on the ground.

Wear long-sleeved shirts to prevent your arms being scraped if you fall or ride under branches.

Wear gloves to give grip on slippery reins and check that the harness on the hat is fastened securely.

Body protectors have special panels designed to absorb impact if you fall.

Correct riding boots help you keep your feet safely in the stirrup irons.

First-aid for rider

All shows should have qualified medical help available. When you arrive at a show, find out where the first-aid base is, in case you need help. If an accident occurs try not to move an injured rider or remove the person's hat, as this may make back or neck injuries worse. Call the first-aiders or paramedics, who will know what to do. Always try to keep calm.

Red Cross volunteers throughout the world are trained to deal with accidents.

Veterinary on call

International competitions have veterinary surgeons in attendance. Organizers of small shows will arrange for a vet to be on call; this means that if a horse is injured, the vet can be contacted and should be there within a short time. Always take a first-aid kit so that you can deal with minor cuts and grazes.

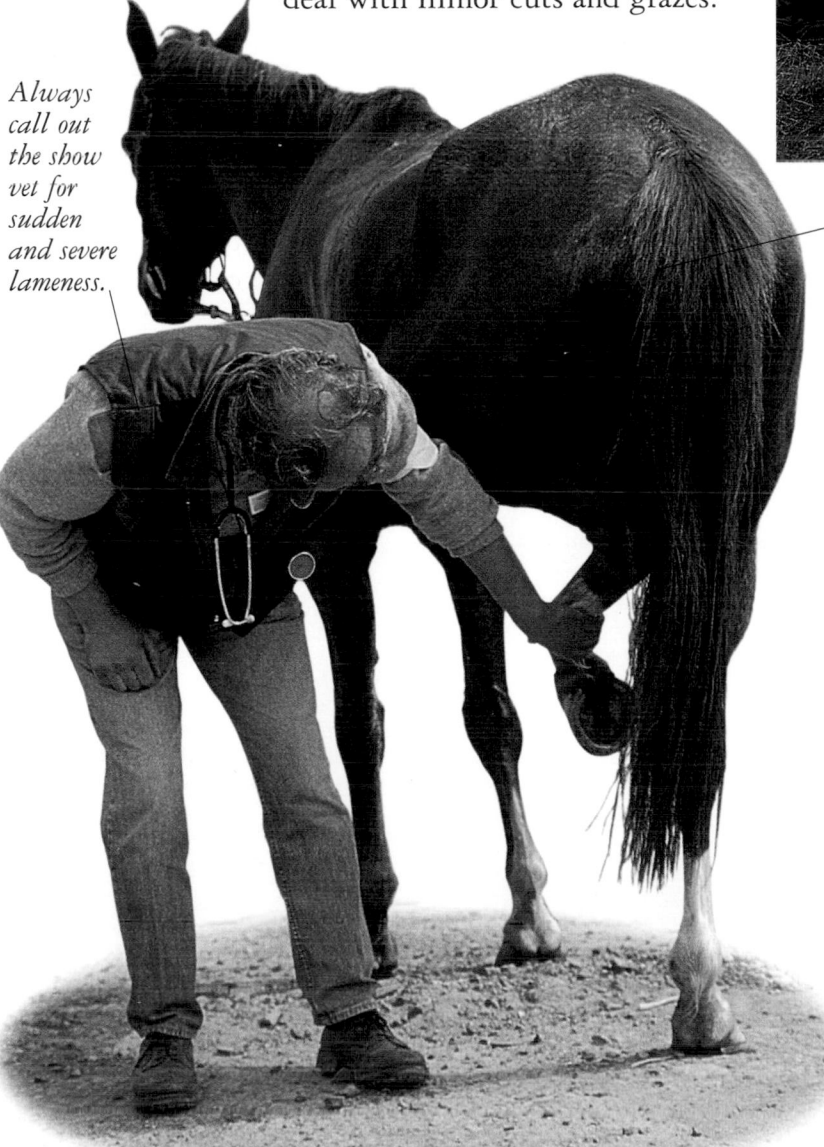

Always call out the show vet for sudden and severe lameness.

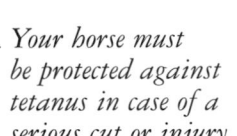

Your horse must be protected against tetanus in case of a serious cut or injury.

Trained first-aiders will know how to prepare an injured rider for safe transport to hospital.

SAFETY CHECKLIST

- When you get to the show, find the first-aid base

- Always make sure your hat harness is fastened before you get on a horse

- Keep protective boots clean and in good repair. Dirty boots may cause skin problems

- Boots cannot be worn for showing or dressage, but you can use them when warming up

- Use studs for competition only, not when riding on the road

Glossary

There are many terms that are used specifically to describe horses, their equipment, and the way that we ride and train them. Listed below are some of the most important and frequently used ones, with a brief explanation of what they mean.

Aids Bodyweight, legs, voice, and hand signals that rider uses to communicate with horse. Martingales, whips and spurs are considered artificial aids.

Backing Teaching a young horse or pony to accept a rider.

Bending race Mounted game in which pony and rider gallop through a row of upright poles.

Blood Used to describe a horse's breeding. A blood horse is another term for a Thoroughbred.

Bounce fences Two fences set at a distance that requires a horse to jump the first, land, then jump the second without a stride in between.

Breastplate Item of tack to help prevent saddle slipping back. Often used for cross-country.

Browband Part of bridle that fits below ears and across top of horse's head; helps keep bridle in place.

Cannon bone The part of the foreleg between the knee and the fetlock.

Canter A three-beat gait that is faster than a trot, but slower than a gallop.

Carriage horse A term used to describe a lightly-built harness horse.

Changing the diagonal Sitting for one beat of a trot, then rising again to adjust the way a horse or pony carries the rider's weight.

Clear round jumping Jumping competition for novice horses or riders where the aim is to jump a clear round over a low course.

Cob Type of riding or driving horse with powerful neck and hindquarters, deep body, and short legs. Show cobs must be over 14.2 hh but not exceed 15.1 hh; only Welsh cobs are a breed.

Coldbloods Another term for heavy horse breeds.

Colic Abdominal pain, which must be treated as an emergency. Signs include kicking or biting at belly, sweating, and pawing ground.

Collecting ring Area at a show where competitors check in before their class. May be used as area to warm up before entering the ring.

Conformation The shape of a horse's body and legs. Good conformation means the horse is well-proportioned.

Cooler Type of rug made from absorbent fabric, which helps to dry a sweating horse.

Crew Back-up team for endurance rider. It meets the horse and rider at stages along the ride to provide food, water, and any help needed.

Crossbreed A horse or pony that is the result of crossing one breed with another breed or type.

Cross surcingles Rug straps, often elasticated and made of nylon, which cross and fasten under a horse's belly to keep rugs in place.

Curry comb Metal or rubber grooming tool used for cleaning brushes. Rubber curry comb can be used to remove dried mud from horse's coat.

Dandy brush Grooming brush with stiff bristles for removing mud and loose hairs from horse's coat.

Dished head A head with a concave profile, such as the Arab.

Double fence Two fences with one or two strides between them; distances must be correct for size of horse.

Dressage training Dressage tests are series of movements to show balance, obedience, and athletic ability of horse, and the partnership between horse and rider.

Endurance riding Sport which involves riding long distances over set course. Distances range from 40–160 km (25–100 miles).

Eventing Dressage, cross-country, and showjumping competition. Also known as horse trials.

Extended strides Action in which a horse or pony takes strides that are as long as possible, without hurrying. Can be in a walk, trot, or canter.

Farrier A person who makes and fits horseshoes.

Feral horse Horse whose ancestors were domesticated, but which now roams in the wild.

Fillers Brightly coloured, solid inserts in show-jumps.

Flat racing Races without jumps for two and three-year-old Thoroughbred horses.

Fly fringe Fringe attached to horse's headcollar, which falls across the face and helps keep flies away.

Forearm The top of the foreleg down to the knee.

Freeze mark A painless security marking system where the horse is cold branded with a unique combination of letters and numbers.

Frog Sensitive V-shaped underneath part of the hoof which acts as a shock absorber.

Gait The pattern of a horse's footsteps.

Gallop A four-beat gait, the fastest pace of all.

Gamgee Padding used under leg bandages, in the stable, or when travelling.

Gelding A male horse that can no longer reproduce.

Girth The measurement around a horse's body where the girth rests.

Gridwork Gymnastic jumping exercises; jumps are set at specific distances to improve horse's athletic skill and confidence, and rider's technique.

Gymkhana Also known as mounted games; requires an athletic pony and rider.

Hacking Riding in the open, either on roads and tracks or across the open countryside.

Hand A unit of measurement to describe a horse's height at the withers. A hand is 10 cm (4 in).

Harness racing Driving races between horses harnessed to light two-wheeled vehicles called sulkies.

HH Abbreviation for hands high.

Hindquarters The back end of a horse, including the hindlegs.

Hocks Powerful joints halfway down the hindleg.

Hotblood Another term for a Thoroughbred or Arab horse or one with a high percentage of Thoroughbred or Arab blood.

Identichipping Form of security marking in which a tiny identichip is injected under the skin. It can be read with a scanner.

Laminitis Serious foot condition, usually linked to pony eating too much rich grass.

Lateral work Dressage and schooling exercises in which horse moves forwards and sideways at the same time.

Leading leg In a canter, a horse or pony takes a longer stride with one foreleg, called the leading leg, than the other.

Lengthened strides The first stage in teaching a horse to extend its paces is to ask for strides that are longer but not faster.

Livery yard Stable yard that provides accommodation for other people's horses and ponies.

Loins The lower part of a horse's back, just in front of the quarters.

Long reining Method of training a young horse or pony to stop, start, and turn before it is ready to accept a rider.

Lungeing 1. Method of training a horse or pony to accept voice commands. 2. Method where an instructor controls a horse or pony during early lessons so the novice rider can concentrate on his or her riding techniques.

Manege An enclosed area used for riding. Also called an arena or an outdoor school.

Mare A female horse more than four years old.

Martingale Piece of tack used to prevent horse putting its head too high; main types are standing, running, and bib martingales.

New Zealand rug Waterproof rug used to keep horse warm in the field.

Noseband Part of bridle that fits across horse's face and fastens above or below the bit, depending on design. Main types include drop, cavesson, Flash, and Grakle.

Over-reach boots Protective boots to help prevent injury if a horse strikes the heel of a front foot with the toe of a back one.

Pasterns The portion of a horse's leg between the fetlock and the hoof.

Pleasure rides Non-competitive rides over distances usually between 16–32 km (10–20 miles).

Points The external parts of a horse that make up its conformation. Also used to describe the tips of the ears, mane, tail, and lower legs.

Poll guard Fastens to headcollar and fits over the poll (top of the horse's head) to protect it when travelling.

Pulling Thinning and shaping horse's mane or tail by pulling out a few hairs at a time.

Quarter marks Designs made with a brush on a show horse's quarters.

Rein back Dressage and schooling exercise in which horse steps backwards. The legs move in diagonal pairs.

Rising trot Where the rider is alternately pushed out of the saddle by a horse's or pony's movement for one beat, then sits for the next.

Serpentine Dressage and schooling exercise in which the aim is to ride loops of equal size and shape – usually three – across the arena.

Showing Classes to show horse's conformation, movement, and manners. Can be ridden or in-hand.

Side reins Reins used to control a horse's or pony's head carriage while it is being lunged.

Stallion A male horse that is used for breeding.

Steeplechasing Races for Thoroughbred horses over brush fences and ditches.

Tack Collective word for saddles, bridles, and other equipment used on riding horses and ponies.

Teeth rasping A process in which sharp edges and "hooks" on horse's teeth are removed using special files by a vet or horse dentist. Teeth must be rasped at least once a year.

Throatlatch (pronounced throatlash). Part of the bridle that fastens under horse's jaw to help keep bridle in place.

Trace clip Type of clip in which hair is removed from lower part of neck and body, following the lines of the traces of a driving harness.

Trail ride or trek A name given to long outdoor rides, often lasting for half a day or a full day.

Trot A two-beat gait in which legs move in diagonal pairs. It is faster than a walk, but slower than a canter.

Trotting up An action in which horse is led at a trot on a straight line, to identify lameness or to demonstrate horse's movement.

Turn on the forehand An exercise where a horse or pony stays in one spot and moves its hindquarters around its front end (forehand).

Vaulting Jumping on to a moving pony without putting feet in the stirrups. An essential skill for mounted games.

Vetgate Compulsory halt during a competitive endurance ride where vet checks horse's soundness, pulse, and respiration.

Vetting Pre-purchase veterinary examination in which vet examines horse for soundness and suitability for a particular purpose.

Warmbloods In general, partbred Arab or Thoroughbred horses. Specifically, there are warmblood breeds such as the Dutch warmblood that have been bred to produce ideal modern sports horses.

Weaving Stable vice in which horse moves its head from side to side.

Weaving grid V-shaped grille that fits on stable door to reduce horse's ability to weave.

Wormer Drugs in paste of granule form that should be given to horses about every six weeks to reduce number of internal worms.

INDEX

fibula 85
field management 49, 51, 76-7
fighting 36, 112
fire precautions 75
first aid
  for horses 38-9, 68-9, 76, 152-3
  for riders 38-9, 74, 153
Fjord 96, 115
flag races 130
flank 42
flat racing 93, 146
flatwork 123
flea-bitten 43
fly fringe 51, 118
food and feeding 38, 48-9, 55, 56-7,
120-1
foot *see* hoof
forage 56, 121
forearm 42
forehand, turning on 28
forelock 42, 60
forward stretch 19
Frederiksborg 101
freeze marking 50
Friesian 104, 115

G
gaited horses 38-9
gaits 14-17, 38-9
galloping 16, 22-3, 108
gates, opening 28, 29, 48
Gelderlander 101
girth
  fastening 9
  tightening 13, 27
gloss, coat 125
grass-kept ponies 45, 48, 49, 50-1, 59,
60, 69, 75, 76, 150
grazing 48-9, 54, 55, 56
grease, leg 126, 143, 152
grey 43, 83
gridwork 31, 120, 121, 139
Groningen 101
grooming 44-5, 55, 58-9, 76-7
  for competition riding 124--5
ground poles 24
group lessons 22-3
gymkhanas 130-1
gymnastic jumping 120

H
habit 132
hack 86
hackamore 32
hacking out 26-7, 36, 38, 120-1, 123
Hackney 109, 114
Haflinger 96-7, 115
half pass 118
hand (measurement) 84
hand signals 27
handling 46-7
Hanoverian 100, 114
harness racing 146, 147
hat or helmet 6, 34, 38, 119, 122, 126,

153
hay 15, 55, 56-7
haynet 56-7, 73
headcollar 46, 50, 51
heavy horse 82, 104-5, 115
heel 42
herdsmen, horses for 110-11
Highland pony 81, 95, 115
hock 42, 43, 84, 85
holes, filling 75
hoof 42, 84, 86
  evolution 80
hoof branding 50
hoof care 44, 45, 55, 58, 62-3, 76-7,
120, 125
hoofpick 27, 38, 45, 58
horse 82-3, 86-7
horse trials *see* eventing
horseball 148, 149
horsebox 72-3, 127, 151
  loading and unloading 37, 72-3
hot blood 82
hunter 86, 87, 114
hunter clip 64

I
Icelandic horse 109, 114
identichipping 50
ill health, signs of 76-7, 120, 121
influenza, equine 76
insects, protection from 50, 51, 118
instructors 6-7
Irish Draught 102, 104, 114

J
jumping 24-5
  advanced 30-1
  clear round 128, 129
  cross-country fences 30, 142-3
  gymnastic 120
  into darkness 143
  saddle 123
  seeing a stride 138
  showjumping 30-1, 102, 118, 138-41

K
kicking 37, 74
knee 42

L
lameness 68, 69, 121
laminitis 49, 69
Landais 97, 115
landing 25
lateral work 28-9
latigo 32
Le Trec 148
lead, giving 28
lead rein 6, 12
leading leg 20
leopard pattern 107
levade 91
light horse 82, 83, 114
Lipizzaner 90, 91, 114

loin 42, 84
lunge rein 6, 12, 34, 121
Lusitano 90, 91, 114

M
mane 42, 60-1
  decorations 107
  plaiting 60, 125, 135, 136
  pulling 60
mane comb 45, 58, 60
manege 15, 22-3
marble pattern 107
markings 43, 83, 107
martingale 17, 135
measuring a horse 84
miniature breeds 98
Moorland pony 94
Mountain pony 94-5, 96
mounted games 130-1
mounting 10
  difficult ponies 37
mounting block 10
muck heap 52
mucking out 45, 53, 55, 77
mule 112
muscle cramp 150
Mustang 112, 114

N
neck reining 32
neckstrap 135
nervous ponies 36
New Forest pony 95, 115
New Zealand rug 66, 67
noseband 9, 123
numnah 71

O
orbit 85
over-reach boots 123, 129, 152
overgirth 152
overo 83, 107

P
pacer 147
Palomino 43, 83, 106, 107
Paso 109, 114
passing side by side 23
pastern 42, 85, 123
Percheron 104, 115
piebald 83, 97, 106
Pinto 106, 107
plaiting 60, 61
  for competition riding 124-5
  dressage 134, 135, 136
points of a horse 42
poisonous plants 48, 51, 75
poll 42
pollguard 73
polo pony 87, 114, 148-9
polocrosse 148
pommel 71
pony 82-3, 86-7, 115
Pony of the Americas 98, 106, 115

ACKNOWLEDGEMENTS

Dorling Kindersley would like to thank the following people whose assistance have made the preparation of this book possible:

CAM Equestrian Ltd, Eardisley, Hereford, for providing images of jumping poles; Lethers, Merstham, Surrey for the loan of equipment and tack. Jackki Garnham and staff, Beechwood Riding School, Woldingham, Surrey; Sandra Waylett, Gatton Park Livery, Reigate, Surrey; Ebbisham Farm Livery Stables, Walton on the Hill, Surrey, for use of their facilities. The show organizers and competitors at Chelsham Riding Club Horse Show, Farleigh, Surrey. The models Holly Clarke, Rosie Eustace, Emma de la Mothe, Kerry Meade, Alison Forrest, and Samantha Wilkinson.

Also thanks to the horses and ponies used in photography and their owners for loaning them. These are: *Cinnamon Dust* (owned by Holly Clarke); *Eliza Doolittle* and *Ginger Pick* (owned by Sandra Waylett); *Peeping Tom* (owned by Maggie Crowley); *Blondie, Tikki, Dillion, Meliton Bay* and *Garochead April* (owned by Jakki Garnham); *Face the Music* (in care of Carolyn Henderson); *Sparkie* (owned by Kerry Meade).

The publishers would also like to thank Ann Barrett for the index and Sarah Goulding for editorial assistance.

The author wishes to acknowledge Elwyn Hartley Edwards for his extensive knowledge of horse and pony breeds.

Picture Credits
The publishers would like to thank the following people for their kind permission to reproduce their photographs:

key: b bottom, c centre, l left, t top, r right

Animal Photography/Sally Anne Thompson: 97br; 103tr;

Bridgeman Art Library, London & N.Y/Roy Miles Gallery, London: 88t (Sir Edwin Landseer, Arab Stallion); **J. Allan Cash Ltd:** 106t; **Bruce Coleman Ltd:** 112bc; **Richard Connor/Glen Tanar Equestrian Centre:** 148t; **John Henderson:** 153t; **Kit Houghton:** 4; 6t; 7; 35tr; 36t; 38b; 45t; 51t; 78; 86-87t; 90t; 110br; 111tl; 109tr; 128b; 131b; 142; 143b; 145b; 146t; 149t, b; 153b; **Bob Langrish:** 26t; 30t; 31t; 35tl; 36bl; 59tr; 64t; 75t, br; 91t; 100br; 102t; 105tr; 108t; 109br; 112t; 113t, br; 116; 118-119; 130b; 131t; 136b; 137b; 140b; 132t; 133t; 141; 143t; 144t, b; 145tl; 146b; 147t, b; 148b; 148-149; **Pictor International:** 33tl; 86t; 111br; **Rex Features:** 60t; **Frank Spooner Pictures:** 89t (Gamma, Alain Benainous); **Tony Stone Images:** 36br.

Additional photography:
Geoff Brightling: 32tr, tl; 32-33; 33br, tl; **Andy Crawford:** 74tr; **Peter Chadwick:** 48 bl; **Kit Houghton:** 15tl, tc; 17tl, tc, tr; 21cl, cc, cr; **Bob Langrish:** 26b; 27tl, tr, br; 45t; 24l; 24-25; 25r; tc, tr; 43cl, c; 49tl; 55tl; 56bl, br; 57bl, bc; 60-61; 65cr; 70bl; 121t, c, b; 122t; **Ray Moller:** 51br; 60tr; **Stephen Oliver:** 45c; **Tim Ridley:** 27bl; 57t; 67tr; 77tr; 121c, 123.
Other photography was taken by: Philip Dowell, Mary Evans, Colin Keates, Karl Shone, Jerry Young, Berwick Woodcuts.

With to all the additional horses and ponies we photographed, and their owners. These are as follows:

Page 42–43: Hippolyte, Haras National de Pau; Montemere O'Nora, Nan Thurman; Oaten Mainbrace, Mr & Mrs Dimmock; Hitman, Boyd Catrell; Foniks, Poul Elmerkjaer.

Page 80–81: Taws Little Buck, Kentucky Horse Park; Fruich of Dykes, Countess of Swindon; Fakir Bola, Moscow Hippodrome, Russia; Murrayton Delphinlis, June Freeman, Murrayton Stud, UK; Hopstone Shabdiz, Mrs Scott, Henden Caspian Stud, UK.

Page 82–83: Hitman, Boyd Cantrell, Kentucky Horse Park, USA.

Page 86–87: Brutt, Robert Oliver, UK; Superted, Robert Oliver, UK; Hobo, Robert Oliver, UK; Amoco Park, Spruce Meadows, Canada (also p92–93).

Page 92–93: Rambling Willie, Farrington Stables & the estate of Paul Siebert; Kentucky Horse Park, USA.

Page 94–95: Barlin, Moscow Agricultural Academy, Russia; Chatsworth Belle; Mrs Hampton, Briar Stud, UK; Fruich of Dykes, Countess of Swinton; Allendale Vampire; Miss M Houlden, Havenstud, UK; Waverhead – William, Mr & Mrs Errington, UK.

Page 96–97: Tressor des Pins, Haras de Pall, France; Ausdan Svcjk, John Goddard Fenwick & Lyn Moran, Dyfed, UK; Orchidea, Sadamo Tombini, Perego, Italy.

Page 98–99: Hopstone Shabdiz, Mrs Scott, Henden Caspian Stud, UK; Pegasus of Kilverstone, Lady Fischer, Kilverstone Wildlife Park, UK; Meriam Beluna, Peltia Jaya Stable, Jakarta, Indonesia; Mels Lucky Boy, Mr D Stewart, Kentucky Horse Park, USA.

Page 100–101: Edison, Mrs Dejonge; Soir d'Avril, Haras Nationaux de l'Isle de Lion d'Angers.

Page 102–103: Miss Mill, Mr R J Lampard; Oaten Mainbrace, Mr & Mrs Dimmock, UK.

Page 104–105: Tango, Haras National de Saint Lo, France; Roy; Kentucky Horse Park, USA.

Page 106–107: Golden Nugget, Sally Chaplin, UK; Laurel Keepsake II, P. Adams and Sons, Laurel Farm, UK.

Page 108–109: Leikner, Kentucky Horse Park, USA; Delights Moondus, Andrew and Jane Shan, Kentucky Horse Park, USA.

Page 110–111: Mr Starpasser, Pat Butcher, Canada; Redonner, Mr Contreras, Les Saintes Maries de la Mer, France.

USEFUL ADDRESSES

Here are the addresses of some associations and other organizations that can help you find out more about horse and pony breeds and riding clubs in your area:

Association of British Riding Schools
Queen's Chambers
38-40 Queen's Street
Penzance
Cornwall TR18 4BH
Tel: 01736 369440

Australian Equine Veterinary Association
PO Box 371
Artarmon
NSW 2064
Australia
Tel: (02) 9411 2733

British Dressage
National Agricultural Centre
Stoneleigh Park
Kenilworth
Warwickshire CV8 2RJ
Tel: 02476 698837

British Horse Society
Stoneleigh Deer Park
Kenilworth
Warwickshire
CV8 2XZ
Tel: 01926 707700

British Horse Trials Association
National Agricultural Centre
Stoneleigh Park
Kenilworth
Warwickshire CV8 2RN
Tel: 02476 698856

British Show Jumping Association
National Agricultural Centre
Stoneleigh Park
Kenilworth
Warwickshire CV8 2LR
Tel: 02476 698800

British Show Pony Society
124 Green End Road
Sawtry
Huntingdon
Cambridgeshire PE28 5XS
Tel: 01487 831376

British Veterinary Association
7 Mansfield Street
London
W1G 9NQ
Tel: 020 7636 6541

Endurance Riding Group
National Agricultural Centre
Stoneleigh Park
Kenilworth
Warwickshire CV8 2RP
Tel: 02476 698863

Equestrian Federation of Australia
196 Greenhill Road
Eastwood
SA 5063
Australia
Tel: (08) 8357 0077

Equestrian Federation Saddle Horse Council
70 Falters Road
Wilberforce
NSW 2756
Australia
Tel: (02) 4575 1341

Farrier Registration Council
Sefton House
Adam Court
Newark Road
Peterborough PE1 5PP
Tel: 01733 319911

National Pony Society
Willingdon House
102 High Street
Alton, Hants
GU34 1EN
Tel: 01420 88333

Ponies Association UK
Chesham House
56 Green End Road
Sawtry
Huntingdon
Cambridgeshire PE28 5UY
Tel: 01487 830278

Pony Club, The
Stoneleigh Deer Park
Kenilworth
Warwickshire
CV8 2XZ
Tel: 01926 707700

Pony Club Association of NSW
PO Box 980
Glebe
NSW 2037
Australia
Tel: (02) 9552 2800

Riding for the Disabled Assoc.
Lavinia Norfolk House
Avenue R
National Agriculture Centre
Stoneleigh Park, Kenilworth
Warwickshire CV8 2LY
Tel: 02476 696510

Society of Master Saddlers, The
Kettles Farm
Mickford
Stowmarket
Suffolk IP14 6BY
Tel: 01449 711642